Renewing the Promise

Renewing the Promise

A Treatise on the Refoundation of the Cameroon Nation

———————————

Julius Nyamkimah Fondong

Spears Books

Denver, Colorado

Spears Books
An Imprint of Spears Media Press LLC
7830 W. Alameda Ave, Suite 103-247
Denver, CO 80226
United States of America

First Published in the United States of America in 2022 by Spears Books
www.spearsmedia.com
info@spearsmedia.com
Information on this title: www.spearsmedia.com/renewing-the-promise

Library of Congress Control Number: 2022940634
ISBN: 9781942876953 (Paperback)
ISBN: 9781942876960 (eBook)

Spears Media Press has no responsibility for the persistence or accuracy of urls for external or third-party internet websites referred to in this publication, and does not guarantee that any content on such websites is, or will remain, accurate or appropriate.

Designed and typeset by Spears Media Press LLC
Cover designed by Doh Kambem

Distributed globally by African Books Collective (ABC)
www.africanbookscollective.com

This book is dedicated to my father, Ba S.A. Fondong, a government accountant who, in my formative years, inculcated in me the values of integrity, personal responsibility, moral probity and accountability in the management of public affairs. These values have defined who I am, and are the backbone of my public stewardship.

Contents

Foreword

In reviewing the crisis of development and democracy in Cameroon, Julius Fondong reflects on the crisis of statehood and development in Africa, using the betrayal of the dreams of prosperity, stability and unity that attended the formation of the Federal Republic of Cameroon in 1961. The book is about Cameroon. But it could also be the story of the betrayal of the Nigerian dream and promise. It could as well be the story of Guinea, Mali, Cote d'Ivoire, or any of the tens of other African countries wrestling with imminent state failure or acute social disorder. These countries are facing both external and internal aggression. They are grappling with extreme poverty as well as extreme social instability. And their myriad socio-economic and political crises seem to derive from the nature of their founding. In a way, one could argue that these countries are founded to fail. Mr. Fondong seeks to understand the nature of this failure and how we can get out of it. By focusing on the Cameroon travails, he deals with some of the main causes of African state failure.

The chief merit of this book is that it reviews a storied history of Cameroon in broad brushes that unearth the reasons for the dysfunction of a promising African country. The theoretical framework of this analysis is universal enough to be applicable to many of Cameroon's neighbors who have come through their political journeys bearing the burden of similar colonial legacy. Some of the analyses hark back to the failure of Cameroonian leaders to deal with what Columbia's renowned anthropologist, Mahmood Mamdani, called 'the legacy of late colonialism'. That is, the failure to reconstruct and reconstitute the illegitimate state structure bequeathed by colonialism. Instead of democratization, we got decentralized dictatorship. The result is that the 'suppressed' 'ethnic' is fighting hard against flawed nation-state. This is the story of Cameroon as well as much of Africa. And even as Fondong captures this universal pathology of the African state order, he properly contextualizes his voice so he can speak meaningfully to the peculiarities of the Cameroonian condition.

With a narration that is mostly controlled, even if sometimes exuberant, scholarly but rooted in practical indices of everyday life, Fondong declares the Cameroonian political project unaccomplished. This lack of accomplishment is not a fait accompli. It could have been avoided. The rest of the book outlines in coherent and simple arguments how the country and its leaders walked themselves into a developmental dystopia. It all started with series of betrayal of promises and breach of trust. What is enlightening in the narrative of these betrayals and breaches is that they can easily map to the crisis of statehood in other African countries, which is a result of failure to conceive the post-colonial African nation-state in a manner that ensures legitimacy and effectiveness. The challenge of statecraft for these states is how to build a state that is both legitimate and effective. Many of the African post-colonial leaders seem to have taken legitimacy for granted and focused on a narrow conception of effectiveness. One manifestation of that oversight was the adoption of one-party states and later, centralization of government under various military and civilian authoritarian regimes. As Fondong relates, one consequence of this administrative misadventure was the collapse of professional and efficient public service leading to the failure of public administration.

Julius Fondong pins the collapse of development and democracy in Cameroon to the failure to keep to the promises made to Cameroonians at independence and later at the renegotiation of the republic. The foremost of these promises is the Promise of Foumban. The Promise of Foumban is typical of the arrangement of post-colonial rule to build multinational African countries that preserve cultural and linguistic differences while anchoring national unity and collective prosperity. This led to federal republics across Africa. The merit of federalism is that it will cater for autochthony without compromising effective strategic actions to achieve prosperity and social development. The concept of African brotherhood points toward a pan-African state and in that wise the various ethnic and religious groups could come together in mutual respect for their freedom and dignity. Cameroon, like its neighbor Nigeria, got off on this footing. As we now know, the federal state arrangement did not guarantee self-determination for the diverse peoples nor engender national unity. Just like the military did in Nigeria in 1966, President Ahidjo, in 1972, dismantled the federal structure and entrenched centralized government with the promise that centralization will banish the ghost of ethnicity, consolidate national unity and free financial resources for national development. Ten years after, Paul Biya promised a new deal based on a different managerial approach that will lead to a professionalized and ethical civil service.

The three promises- two structural and one managerial- all failed to deliver.

Today, Cameroon has not been able to reach its full potentials as the human development indicators will show. It remains a poor country, and the peaceful agitations for self-determination have turned violent, leading to the specter of a possible civil war or even worse. The country is in tribulation. The Southern Cameroons question has not been answered. The Anglo-Cameroon question is yet unanswered. As usual, the ruling elites are diffident, halfhearted, and insincere, trying to solve a structural problem without altering the foundations of the republic.

There is nothing new about the narrative of failure and misgovernance in many of the African countries. But what is different about the approach of the book is the connection between failure of state formation and management of state institutions of service delivery. With evidence-based analysis, the author connects the structural and managerial aspects of state failure. He argues for a re-founding of the republic on the basis of a sincere recognition of the diversity of the peoples of Cameroon and robust institutionalization of a structure of governance that enforces the right of Southern Cameroons to self-determination. At the same time, he recognizes that recovering a viable state from the debris of Cameroon is not just about restructuring the superstructure of the political economy. It must involve reform of public service to entrench professionalism and a new culture of efficient service delivery, based on the principle of the New Public Administration. This is beyond tokenistic neoliberal reform. It is about regaining the effectiveness of the state.

The trick in solving the Cameroonian crisis is walking through the narrow corridor of self-determination without resorting to secessionist enterprises that have become the easy resort of a disoriented political class that fails to understand the new realities of the post-colonial African state. As Fondong rightly observes, Cameroon today is not Cameroon of the 1960s. We cannot make a clean break of the webs of relationship between ethnic and social groups. We have to recreate the state in the light of the contingencies and ambiguities of contemporary times, and not reinvent it in the sentiment of primordiality. We need a state that works. The only way the state can work is if it is constituted to provide economic and political freedoms and fits into the complexities of lived existence.

The book is not a tale of woes. It offers a solution to the pathology of a failing state. It recommends the trinity of decentralization of power, reformation of the public service and reinvention of political leadership from incompetent, autocratic, and transactional model to transformative, audacious, and right-respecting model. Many books on transformation of the troubled African state usually either settle on the imperative or a new political leadership or new state institution. The genius of the book is that it combines the institutional and managerial paradigms for the recreation of a new Cameroon republic, consistent with the Promise of Foumban.

The book recommends audacity for political leadership in Cameroon. It takes its own pill. I am delighted that in spite of the author's obvious identification with the agitations of the people of Southern Cameroons, he rejects that the solution lies in insurrectional ethno-regional agitation or secession. Rather, he sees the answer in a broad-based democratic struggle to recreate the state that gives every citizen, every social and ethnic group, the right to self-determination. This is what I call 'democratic citizenship'. The premise is that the solution to Africa's state malformation lies in more and not less democracy. It also lies in better technocracy, the type that creates more and better goods and services, one that reduces the deadly fight over varnishing resources.

If the leaders of Cameroon will take these words to heart, if African leaders steadying the crumbling edifices of the post-colonial nation-states can take these words to heart, then we might be on the path to rebuilding sustainable new African states that can secure the promises of peace, prosperity, and justice to all their people. This book is a guiding-light for getting to that future.

Dr Sam Amadi
Associate Professor of Law and President,
Abuja School of Social and Political Thought, Abuja, Nigeria
September 2021

Preface

In December 2016, I visited with Professor Emeritus and author, Anthony Ndi, at his residence at Foncha Street, Bamenda, Cameroon. As we sat and talked, our conversation soon turned to Cameroon politics. At that time, Bamenda was in full revolutionary effervescence, marked by strikes and demonstrations organized by lawyers to protest what they said were attempts by the government to undermine the common law system that obtains in Anglophone Cameroon. They were also demanding an end to Anglophone Cameroon marginalization. A month before, precisely on 21 November 2016, a local FM Radio host by name Mancho Bibixy had led a demonstration of mostly young people through the streets of Bamenda to protest against the inability of the Bamenda City Council to provide its citizens with the most basic of services such as safe drinking water and good roads. Addressing thousands of protesters while standing in an open coffin, Mr Bibixy declared that he was prepared to die in his crusade to ensure that the City Council was responsive to the needs of the people. This was what came to be known as the "Coffin Revolution". Before long, the Coffin Revolution had gone from a demand for better municipal services to popular protests against Anglophone Cameroon marginalization, thus aligning itself to the demands of the lawyers.

In a desperate attempt to stem the tide of protests that was sweeping across the City of Bamenda, and in an effort to regain control of the fast deteriorating situation, leaders of the ruling Cameroon People's Democratic Movement (CPDM) organized a counter march in Bamenda on 8 December 2016 ostensibly to show support to their National President and Head of State, President Paul Biya. The idea of the counter-march incensed the youths who again took to the streets in their thousands determined to stop it. In the crackdown that ensued, some of the demonstrators were shot and killed by security forces and public and private property were destroyed. A coalition of teachers and lawyers associations soon emerged and a full-fledged civil resistance campaign was in gestation. The teachers and lawyers were now out-rightly demanding a return to the pre-1972 federal structure as the only way of ending Anglophone Cameroon marginalization.

As Professor Ndi and I analyzed these events and what may follow, we shared worrisome concerns about the dark path towards which the country seemed to be gliding. We exchanged ideas as to what we believed needed to be done to rescue the country. At that point, Prof Ndi turned to me and practically ordered me to write a book. "Let a thousand flowers blossom", I think he said. It was in that moment that the idea of this book started forming in my mind.

But it was not only Professor Ndi's injunction that spurred me to action. All my children are currently living and studying out of Cameroon. Even though they all have different nationalities, they have remained deeply attached to their Cameroonian roots. By 2018 the civil disobedience campaign in Anglophone Cameroon, led by the teachers and lawyers, had morphed into an armed conflict. The conflict had acquired a level of savagery and barbarity hitherto unknown and it was making headline news on all major international news networks. I was visiting with my children in the U.S. at the time. As we talked over dinner one evening, the violence in Cameroon came up.

My daughter, who was eleven years old at the time, looked at me straight in the face and asked me "Daddy what are you doing about the war in Cameroon? Shall we ever be able to go back again to Bali on vacation?" My heart sank. I didn't have a ready response for her.

However, I realized at that point I needed to get involved, in one way or the other, in the search for a peaceful solution to the violence afflicting the only homeland I have, and which I proudly share with my children. Even though this book is not solely about the violent conflict in Anglophone Cameroon, it was clearly inspired by it.

The armed conflict that broke out in Anglophone Cameroon in 2017 is not an isolated singularity. It is the expression of a general malaise and a reprehensible state of affairs that have beleaguered the nation since unification in 1961, but which have largely been ignored, minimized, underestimated and left unattended. There is a running joke among Cameroonians, namely that, if someone explains Cameroon to you and you say you have understood, it means you have not. The implication here is that Cameroon, as a socio-political construct, is some sort of a sphinx-like creature or an unfathomable phenomenon whose mere existence defies natural logic; or that Cameroon as a polity cannot be rationally defined and therefore exist outside the realms of human comprehension. None of this is true. It may just be a joke, but it is also a lazy attempt to push all the nation's problems under the carpet by believing that they are inscrutable and therefore unidentifiable and unsolvable. This nation's failures, shortcomings and structural problems are well-known and have been well articulated for years. In fact, over the years, President Paul Biya himself has at different times identified corruption, inertia and administrative bottlenecks as the triple malevolence holding this country back. Ideas, strategies, programs and recommendations on how to adequately address them also abound. What is lacking is the courage, the political will and the quality of political leadership needed to implement them.

The year 2021 marked the sixtieth anniversary of the unification of the independent Republic of Cameroon (or French Cameroun) and the self-governing territory of Southern Cameroons (or British Cameroons) to form the Federal Republic of Cameroon. The country has gone through different mutations during this time. A "Peaceful Revolution" in 1972 abrogated the Federal system which was the foundational governing system agreed upon in 1961; changes in the official appellation of the country (from "Federal Republic of Cameroon" to the "United Republic of Cameroon" to the "Republic of Cameroon") have also elicited changes in the form of the state. The nation has gone from a two-state federation to an overly centralized, Jacobin, 10-region unitary state model, in which power is concentrated in an Executive Presidency. In the process, citizen's voice and participation in the decision-making process have been stymied, corruption has become endemic, civil liberties have been grossly curtailed, and the political space is shrinking by the day as the State becomes more and more repressive and over-bearing. In addition, the country seems to be in what Dr Sam Amadi calls a "developmental dystopia", almost incapable of matching the pace of public service delivery to the ever-increasing needs of a burgeoning population. Clan politics and the confiscation of power by an increasingly intolerant political elite have led to the weakening and to the capture of the institutions of State. National Unity and National Integration have not gone deep enough as the country is far more fragile, less inclusive and less united today than it was six decades ago.

This is where I believe the nation is after sixty years of unification.

Sixty years is a relatively long time in the life of nation. It took the Chinese half that time to go from a primeval, agrarian society to a high-tech, industrialized economy, and in the process lifted more than 500 million of their people out of extreme poverty. Similarly, it has taken Rwanda half of that time to go from a "non-state" ravaged by genocide, to one of the fastest growing and one of the best transforming economies on the African continent. So, sixty years is more than enough time for a nation to find itself and define its path to the future. It is also the time for introspection and stock-taking on the road so far covered.

This is what I primarily set out to do in this book. In writing this treatise, I hope to start a genuine conversation on the state of this nation, six decades after unification. I proceed from the contention that all modern nation-states were founded on a promise. For the Americans, for example, it was a promise to forge a nation-state respectful and protective of the inalienable right of its citizens to "life, liberty and the pursuit of Happiness". Similarly, during its liberation struggle and after taking over power in 1994, the African National Congress (ANC) pledged and promised to build a multiracial, democratic post-Apartheid South Africa, based on the principle of one person one vote.

Cameroon as a nation-state was founded on a promise of its own. When the leaders of *La Republique du Cameroun* and those of Southern Cameroons met in Foumban in July 1961 to lay the foundations of a new nation-state, a promise emerged from that meeting. This is what I have termed in this treatise "The Promise of Foumban". It was a promise to build a unique post–colonial, Cameroon nation-state, federal in character but united in its diversity and in purpose; proud of its bicultural heritage derived from the distinct colonial, historical and cultural realities of each of the two parts of the union. In the Constitution that was adopted to crystalize this promise, the leaders pledged that the Federal Republic of Cameroon shall be "democratic, secular and dedicated to social service; it shall ensure the equality before the law of all its citizens". A promise of this nature is essentially a social contract between the government and the governed. And a nation is only as good as its promises.

The unique nature of promises, especially those of a national political character, is that they must remain immune to changing circumstances. For foundational promises to be worth their salt, they must be unfazed by the vagaries of a psychedelic socio-political landscape such as Cameroon is. Yet, over the years actions have been taken, and decisions have been made - sometimes with naked arrogance - which have amounted to brazen travesties of the founding promise of this nation: The Promise of Foumban. The abrogation of the federal system in 1972 (with the promise that it shall result in net budgetary gains that shall be ploughed back into development of programs) and the change of the appellation of the State in 1983 (as part of the Promise of the New Deal that it would enhance national integration), are examples of such travesties. The Cameroon nation is today dangling dangerously on a nervous precipice, and risking an implosion at any time, largely because its founding promise was never fulfilled. As a nation we seem to be on a wrong course, and have been so for a long time. There is therefore an urgent need for course-correction. This is the second objective of this treatise.

After analyzing the nation's performance as reported in some internationally acclaimed indexes, the Cameroon Government's own reports and reports of its bilateral partners, I come to the conclusion that the country has not made significant progress in its socio-economic development efforts over the past three decades. Nevertheless, since the objective here is not just about appraising government performance, I go one step further to make broad-based policy recommendations on what I believe can be done to put the nation back on track. The recommendations are essentially governance-based. They are drawn from my biased position of a governance expert and a public policy analyst. These recommendations come from my deep conviction that progress, change and innovation in a nation are largely determined by the quality and the strength of that nation's institutions, and by the manner in which its leaders exercise authority and leverage political power.

A combination of underperforming institutions, abuse of authority and ham-fisted and arrogant leadership has had a deleterious, but also, a lethargic effect on this nation, for most of its history as an independent state. In this book, therefore, I argue that taking Cameroon to the next step in its history should begin with the renewal of the promise on which it was founded. In this regard I offer an overarching praxis for the refoundation of the Cameroon nation predicated on the principles of decentralized governance, innovative public service delivery and transformational leadership. This is my case for the refoundation of the Cameroon nation and for the renewal of its promise.

Writing this book would never have been possible without the encouragements, gentle prodding, insistence and support of a whole lot of people.

I am grateful to Prof Ndi, not only for giving me the inspiration to write this book, but also for taking time off his busy schedule to review the manuscript and offer constructive criticism. My lifelong friends, Divine Nchamukong, Dr Gomia Victor, Prof Jerry J.K. Dohmatob and Dr Jude Fokwang have for years been on my case, relentlessly prodding me to publish my thoughts. To them I say thank you for jolting me out of my languor. In a very special way I wish to thank Dr Jude Fokwang for reviewing the initial chapters of the book and offering valuable suggestions, and also for accepting to publish it.

My sincere gratitude also goes to Mr Tohmoh Joseph, Senior Adviser in the Ministry of Basic Education, Cameroon, for providing me with instructive insights into PASEC and UAS assessment frameworks. Those insights were critical to my understanding of the government's policy towards the attainment of quality, Universal Primary Education. In that same vein I extend my immense gratitude to Mr. Alfred Tendo for sharing with me his notes on Pa

Yasom Tondo's contribution towards the development of fresh water fishing in Cameroon. I also wish to thank Justice Nchang Augustin Amongwa for reviewing parts of Chapter Three and offering critical advice on my proposals for the judicial enforcement of municipal laws.

This book may not have seen the light of day without the assistance of Ms. Saba Di Roberto and Mr. Babila Tanyi, who acted as my unpaid research assistants, helping to collect, collate and analyze hundreds of pages of data from a myriad of sources. To both of them, I say a huge thank you.

I also wish to extend special appreciation to my daughter, Ms. Vanessa Ngum, an undergraduate student in Computer Sciences at the University of Witwatersrand, who in spite of her own charged academic schedule, took the time to proof-read the entire manuscript. In the process, she was able to pick out some spelling and syntactical errors I had overlooked. In her characteristic perceptiveness, she challenged some of my assumptions, demanded more clarity on certain points and generally weaned me of my compulsion to start a sentence with conjunctions. Her efforts have made this book infinitely better than it otherwise could have been.

Profound gratitude goes to my entire family, especially my children, who had to endure my absence, my silence and sometimes my different mood swings as I grappled to complete this work, in the midst of a raging pandemic. I could afford to take these liberties only because my wife, Mamon Nahsang Gladys Bibi-Fondong, was always there to give me the strength and the assurance I needed to trudge along, even when I felt like giving up. I am also grateful to her for providing me with critical insights into the structure and functioning of the education system in South Africa, with special regard to the relationship between the schools, Education Districts and the Department of Education. In spite of her own crowded schedule, she also managed to find the time (in a way only she can) to read through parts of the manuscript and offer some editing tips.

To all others who contributed in one way or the other towards the writing and publication of this book, I give a huge thank you.

I wrote this book when I was still a serving staff member of the United Nations. So it is reasonable to surmise that I may have been influenced by time-tested U.N values, principles and doctrines, especially those that relate to the right to self-determination and the peaceful resolution of conflicts. I must however, stress that the views and positions expressed herein are solely mine and do not in any manner, shape or form represent the official views or position of the United Nations.

Goma, June 2022

List of Abbreviations

BBC	British Broadcasting Cooperation
CAP	Certificat d'Aptitude Professionelle
CBS	Columbia Broadcasting System
CFA	*Communauté Financière Africaine*
CNU	Cameroon National Union
ECAM	Enquête *Camerounaise* Auprès des Ménages
EIU	Economist Intelligence Unit
ENAM	Ecole Nationale de l'Administration et de la Magistrature
FENASCO	Fédération National des Sports Scolaires et Universitaire
FSI	Fragile State Index
GCE	General Certificate of Education
GDP	Gross Domestic Product
GESP	Growth and Employment Strategy Paper
GNI	Gross National Income
GPE	Global Partnership for Education
GPS	Government Primary School
HDI	Human Development Index
HIPC	Heavily Indebted Poor Countries
IGERA	Inspection Générale de la Réforme Administrative
IIAG	Ibrahim Index of African Governance
IMF	International Monetary Fund
KUC	Kumbo Urban Council
KWA	Kumbo Water Authority
MDG	Millennium Development Goals
M&E	Monitoring and Evaluation
MoU	Memorandum of Understanding
NDS30	National Development Strategy 30

NPM	New Public Management
PASEC	Program d'Analyse des Systèmes Educatifs de la CONFEMEN
PCR	Primary Completion Rate
PNEU	Parents National Education Union
PRSP	Poverty Reduction Strategy Paper
PTA	Parents Teacher Association
SAP	Structural Adjustment Plan
SCNC	Southern Cameroons National Council
SDF	Social Democratic Front
SDG	Sustainable Development Goals
SNEC	Société Nationale des Eaux du Cameroun
SSA	Sub Saharan Africa
TAC	Teachers Association of Cameroon
UAE	United Arab Emirates
UAS	Unité d'Acquis Scolaire
UNDP	United Nations Development Program
UNFPA	United Nations Fund for Population Activities
UNO	United Nations Organization
WEF	World Economic Forum
WHO	World Health Organization
WOCCU	World Council of Credit Unions

For one true measure of a nation is its success in fulfilling the promise of a better life for each of its members. Let that be the measure of our nation.

John F. Kennedy

Chapter One

Introduction: Promises Broken, Trust Betrayed

The 1980s BBC's political satire sitcom, "Yes, Minister" is without doubt one of the most popular TV shows in recent memory. Its popularity lies in the fact that it exposed the inner workings of government for all to see, in a way that no show before it had been able to do. In nominating "Yes, Minister", as Britain's Best Sitcom of all times, journalist, Armando Iannucci said thanks to the show, the British public came to know that their country was not being run, as the word "run' would suggest some activity or some level of mobility. Rather, Iannucci averred, the country was being expertly kept at a standstill by bumbling politicians and devious bureaucrats.[1] I often wonder if the same thing is not happening in present day Cameroon.

A National Dream Deferred

Cameroon is a country in the Central African sub region with a population of 26 million spread over 475,000 km². The country is often described as "Africa in Miniature" because it is imbued with virtually all the geographical and socio-cultural features of the continent: dry northern savanna, lush equatorial rain forest of the South, a complex ethno-linguistic structure, significant influences of Christianity, Islam and African Religions etc. In addition, the country is blessed with an abundance of natural resources notably, timber, oil, gas, an assortment of minerals, a rich coastline ideal for the development of ports and tourism, and above all else, enormous human resource potentials. Ideally, the country has all it takes to become a rich, prosperous and progressive nation.

Unfortunately the country seems to be at a standstill. It looks like the nation is being diligently kept at a dead end by an entrenched political hegemony, bereft

---

1   BBC Documentary "Britain's Best Sitcom – Yes Minister", written and narrated by Armando Iannucci, posted on YouTube on 27th December 2010.

of any novel ideas on how to move the country forward, but which is either too proud to know it or too scared to admit it. If we cast a cursory look at the last thirty years, it is difficult to point to any significant, ground-breaking progress made in any sector of national life - health, education, economic development, governance, democratic freedoms, exercise of public liberties, infrastructure etc. Simply put, the nation is struggling to live up to its avowed dream and vision of building a "land of promise" and a" land of glory" as proclaimed in the refrain of its National Anthem.

But lest we forget, Cameroon as a post-colonial nation-state was built and took shape on a number of promises. I shall call these promises The Promise of Foumban, The Promise of 20 May 1972 and The Promise of the New Deal.

The Promise of Foumban and the Foundation of a Nation-State

On 11 February 1961, the British-administered United Nations Trust Territory of Southern Cameroons overwhelmingly voted in a plebiscite to achieve independence by joining the French speaking la *Republique du Cameroun*. French Cameroon, as it was also called, had gained independence from France on 1 January 1960.

Pursuant to the 11 February Plebiscite results, leaders of *la Republique du Cameroon* led by President Ahmadou Ahidjo and those of Southern Cameroons led by Premier John Ngu Foncha met in the town of Foumban from the 17-21 of July 1961 in a conference. The objective of that conference was for both sides to discuss and agree on the terms of their union and to transcribe this agreement into a Constitution. The new Constitution which was fashioned out of the Foumban Conference and other tripartite meetings that were subsequently held between Ahidjo, Foncha, and the administering authorities, was federal in character. It is important to emphasize that that Constitution, which went into effect on 1 October 1961 (the day the new, unified nation was born), created a federation of two equal states.

A lot has been said and written about the Foumban Conference, especially from Anglophone Cameroon nationalists. Some of these nationalists affirm that Foumban was a hoax; that the Southern Cameroons delegation was ill-prepared and blindsided; that Ahidjo showed an abundance of bad faith. These are all legitimate concerns and maybe on hindsight, they needed to have been addressed so as establish the basis of mutual trust, which is an essential ingredient in the kind of noble enterprise on which leaders of both territories had embarked.

Its shortcomings notwithstanding, a promise emerged out of Foumban. It was the promise to build a unique postcolonial, Cameroon nation-state, federal in character but united in its diversity and purpose; proud of its bicultural heritage derived from the distinct colonial, historical and cultural realities of each of the two parts of the union. It was also a promise ostensibly made in the spirit of true brotherhood. The banner hanging over the heads of the leaders as they sat on the table to forge out a new nation proclaimed:

HOW NICE IT IS TO MEET OUR BROTHERS. VIVE LE CAMEROUN UNIFIE

Such a promise could only have been inspired by a profound nationalist fervor analogous to that expounded in Gellner's social anthropological views of nationhood.

In his 1983 seminal work *Nations and Nationalism,* Ernest Gellner describes two ways in which a nation comes into being. First, a nation is formed, Gellner argues, if and only if the people share the same culture. Gellner understands culture as a system of ideas and signs and associations and ways of behaving and communicating. And second, an entity is recognized as a nation if and only if its people recognize each other as belonging to the same nation.[2] These two ingredients, especially the first, may not have been fully present in Foumban but that did little to dampen the enthusiasm of the leaders of the two territories.

The political entity known as Cameroon is the outcome of German colonialism. It was the Germans, who after the Berlin Conference of 1884, carved out a colony for themselves in the heart of Africa, stretching from the shores of Lake Chad in the North through the dense equatorial forest in the South and Southwest to the grassfield regions that shared borders with the British colony of Nigeria to the East. In the process, the German colonial state of Kamerun brought together different sociological components comprising some 230 diverse ethno-linguistic groups, Muslims, Christians, Animists etc. After the defeat of the Germans in the First World War, and pursuant to article 22 of the Covenant of the League of Nations that came into effect on 28 June 1919, the German colony of Kamerun became a League of Nations Mandated Territory. It was placed under the administration of the French and the British, with the French getting two thirds of the colony and the remaining third going to the British. With the creation of the United Nations Organization (U.N.O.) in October 1945, and the setting up of its Trusteeship Council, the colony of Cameroon became a U.N. Trust Territory under the same arrangements as existed under

2   Gellner, E. (1983). *Nations and Nationalism.* Oxford: Basil Blackwell Publisher Limited. P.7

the League of Nations Mandate. The colony thus remained divided along those lines till unification on 1 October 1961.

Professor Ali Mazuri professed in his instructive documentary "The Africans: A Triple Heritage" that one of the enduring legacies of Europe's colonization of Africa was that it brought together people who otherwise should have been separate and separated people who otherwise should have been together.[3]

In a sense the Foumban Conference was borne out of the desire to put back together what history had put asunder. Foumban was both an affirmation of a shared historical experience and the recognition of the common bonds of brotherhood that bind, or should henceforth bind, the peoples of those two territories, to wit, *La Republique du Cameroon* and Southern Cameroons. The common denominator here was of course "Cameroon" in all its ramifications.

It is within this context that 1 October 1961 should be understood. The significance of 1 October 1961 is not just the day the British-administered United Nations Trust Territory of Southern Cameroons gained its independence by joining the already independent *La Republique du Cameroon*. It was something much bigger and seemingly inscrutable.

On 1 October 1961 a sovereign country and a self-governing autonomous territory did something, which at the time was unusual and almost without precedent in contemporary African political history. *La Republique du Cameroun*, renounced its independence and sovereignty attained on 1 January 1960 and entered into a union with Southern Cameroons, an autonomous, self-governing territory with a flourishing democratic culture since 1954, and they both assumed the status of federated states in a union of equal partners. That is the mystique of 1 October 1961.

In the Constitution that defined the terms of their union they proclaimed that:

> The Federal Republic of Cameroon shall be democratic, secular and dedicated to social service; it shall ensure the equality before the law of all its citizens; and it proclaims its adherence to the fundamental freedoms written into the Universal Declaration of Human Rights and the Charter of the United Nations.[4]

---

3   "The Africans: A Triple Heritage" is a documentary history, written and narrated by Dr. Ali Mazrui in the early 1980s and jointly produced by the BBC and the Public Broadcasting Service (WETA, Washington) in association with the Nigerian Television Authority.
4   Constitution of the Federal Republic of Cameroon, Promulgated into law on September 1, 1961 by Ahmadou Ahidjo President of la Republique du Cameroun, Section 1.2.

That was their promise to their peoples and to the world. The Promise of Foumban had been crystalized.

The Promise of 20 May 1972

On 20 May 1972, at the behest of President Ahidjo, a referendum was organized in which Cameroonians were asked to vote for or against the continued existence of the Federation. Cameroonians overwhelming voted to abolish the Federation. Pursuant to the results of the referendum the Federation was abolished in favor of a unitary state. In moving to end the Federal Republic, Mr. Ahidjo (one of the main architects of the Promise of Foumban) argued that the federal state structure, with its three governments, four assemblies and three civil services was too costly for the new nation. Resources that should be going into development programs and into the nation building effort were being spent to support a very heavy and cumbersome state apparatus. Therefore it was time to do away with the federation, so as to free up resources in favor of national development. On the face of it the arguments made sense. But the change of the form of the state could also fundamentally imperil *the principles* and the Promise of Foumban: union of equal partners, unity in diversity, one state two systems.

The country thus changed its official appellation from the "Federal Republic of Cameroon" to the "United Republic of Cameroon". All federal institutions as well as the institutions of the federated states were dissolved. Even though this amounted to an overt violation of the Promise of Foumban, it was thought then that the word "United" in the new appellation of the State implied a tacit recognition that the country was borne of a union of two entities. And so in a sense, The Promise of Foumban was still alive. Or was it?

It is important to recall here that in moving to abolish the federation, President Ahidjo promised that national unity shall be consolidated and the financial gains that shall accrue therefrom shall be used to invest in development projects across the country. That was The Promise of 20 May 1972.

There was going to be another promise. I shall call this third promise The Promise of the New Deal.

The Promise of the New Deal

On 6 November 1982, President Ahmadou Ahidjo resigned the presidency and handed over power to his constitutional heir and Prime Minister, Mr. Paul Biya. The 49-year-old Mr. Biya had largely served in Ahidjo's shadow for twenty years. He was very unassuming and a political lightweight by all counts. He was thought to be naïve, unambitious and still beholden to his mentor, Ahmadou

Ahidjo. His credentials were that of a bureaucrat, not of a hard-nosed politician.

So when Mr. Biya addressed the nation from the rostrum of the National Assembly in the morning of 6 November1982 for the first time as the newly sworn-in President and Head of State, he sounded refreshingly different from his predecessor, who was known to make long, politically-charged speeches. He focused his address on governance and public administration, not politics (after all he wasn't a politician). He promised to Cameroonians the dawn of a new era. He called this new era the New Deal. This New Deal was going to be anchored on the values of integrity, rigor and moralization in the management of public affairs. In this regard, the new President vowed to do away with the administrative and bureaucratic bottlenecks that had made of the Cameroonian public administrative system heavy, inept and underperforming. He challenged his fellow country men and women to shun irregularities, lateness, laxity, and irresponsibility. The President urged Cameroonians to condemn and desist from the misappropriation of public funds, corruption, fraud, illicit acquisition of wealth and moral depravity.[5]

On 9 February 1983, the new President paid his maiden visit to Bamenda, headquarters of the Anglophone North-West Province, barely three months after assuming the Presidency. I was among the thousands of people who turned up at the Bamenda Municipal Stadium to listen to the President speak. Addressing the enthusiastic crowd in English (the first time a President had ever done so), President Biya again harped on his favorite theme of the urgent need for administrative reform as the cornerstone of the New Deal he had promised Cameroonians three months earlier when he took office. He drew prolonged applause from the crowd when he declared that he shall put an end to the costly trips made to the political capital city of Yaoundé for the purpose of "chasing files".

The Bamenda visit was of strategic importance to the President. It instantly won him the trust and the support of the Anglophone minority. His emphasis on public service and civil service reform resonated well with the people. And so, a sizzling honeymoon began between the Anglophone population and the new President. But that trust began to erode and the honey moon started fading away when the President undertook to change the official appellation of the state, without proper consultation and with little regard for the legal and political implications it will have on the status of Anglophones within the Cameroon polity. At that point, Anglophone Cameroonians were asking themselves what

---

5   Ngoh, V. J. (2019). *Cameroon 1884-Present (2018): The History of a People*. Limbe: Design House. p. 202.

the Promise of the New Deal meant for them. Was it just a mirage or was it going to turn out to be a Raw Deal?

From "United" Republic back to "The Republic"

On 4 February 1984, President Biya promulgated Law No.84-1, changing the name of the country from the "United Republic of Cameroon" to the "Republic of Cameroon". In doing so, the President and his political ideologues argued that national unity had already been attained and was no longer relevant to the New Deal Agenda and its promises. What the country needed, they opined, was "national integration" and better inclusion. The change of the official appellation of the country from "United Republic of Cameroon" to "The Republic of Cameroon" was meant to signify this change in national priorities. In making this change, Mr. Biya was obviously trying to diverge from his predecessor with whom he had fallen out in the meantime. He was thus striving to assert himself by rebranding the country.

It is important to remember that "Republic of Cameroon" (or *La Republique du Cameroun*) was the name under which French Cameroon gained independence on 1 January1960. It had given up that name on 1 October 1961, to become the federated state of "East Cameroon" in the Federal Republic of Cameroon; in the same way that Southern Cameroons had given up that appellation to become the federated state of "West Cameroon". In changing the name of the state in such a cavalier manner, Mr. Biya, wittingly or unwittingly, had destroyed a foundational principle of The Promise of Foumban. By taking away the 'United" from the "United Republic of Cameroon" Mr. Biya had also taken away the raison d'etre of any continued union between the two polities that came together to create a post-colonial nation-state called Cameroon.

How have the Promises Fared?

It is often said that a nation is only as good as its promises. So, six decades after unification, how have the *Promise of Foumban*, the *Promise of 20 May 1972*, and the *Promise of the New Deal* fared? Have they achieved their objectives of building a unique nation-state, prosperous, united in its diversity and respectful of its dual colonial heritage? Have we been able to build a truly democratic nation in which all are equal before the law and in which public affairs are managed with rigor and moralization? Did the abrogation of the Federation lead to greater consolidation of national unity? And did it result in net financial gains that were ploughed back into socio-economic development projects, evenly implemented in a fair and equitable manner all over the national territory? Has national integration created inclusiveness and a protuberant sense of national belonging?

Unfortunately it is hard to answer to any of these questions in the affirmative. Sixty years after unification, Cameroon seems to be a divided, fractious, fragile, pseudo-state dangling dangerously on a nervous precipice, seemingly risking an implosion at any time.

Political Inconsideration and the Exacerbation of Anglophone Grievances

A ferocious, savage, armed conflict is raging in Anglophone Cameroon, after armed wings of a separatist movement emerged in 2017. At the root of this conflict is the abolition of the Federation in 1972 and the renaming of the country in 1984.

The Federation offered a veneer of guarantee for the political and administrative autonomy and the preservation of the way of life of the country's Anglophone minority. Soon after unification in 1961, the government in Yaoundé started a policy of so-called "harmonization". Though it was never openly said, it would appear harmonization was intended to totally absorb and assimilate the Anglophone minority into the Francophone majority. This has resulted in the effective marginalization of Anglophone Cameroonians, who now believe they have become second class citizens in what was supposed to be a union of two equal partners. This is what has come to be known as the *Anglophone Problem*.

The Anglophone Problem has its corollary, the Southern Cameroons Question. The Southern Cameroons Question has as one of its proximate causes, the change of the official appellation of the state from the "Federal Republic of Cameroon" to the "United Republic of Cameroon" and then to he "Republic of Cameroon". All these changes, often made in a cavalier and inconsiderate manner, have had profound legal and political implications for the status of Anglophone Cameroonians within the national polity.

The political and legal implications of these name changes have been well articulated by dedicated and erudite Anglophone Cameroon nationalists like Dr Simon Munzu (a legal scholar and a former United Nations Secretary-General's Deputy Special Representative) but most emphatically by Barrister Gorji Dinka (a prominent lawyer and former president of the Cameroon Bar Council).

In an open letter addressed to President Biya dated 20/03/1985 Barrister Gorji Dinka, argued that:

> By reviving the old Republic of Cameroun, which the Foumban Accord
> had submerged in order to create a Federation with Southern Cam-
> eroons-on-Ambas, the Republic of Cameroun has irretrievably well

seceded from the union. So, unless a new Accord is concluded so as to create a basis for the union between the two States, any claim by the Republic of Cameroun to govern Southern Cameroons-on-Ambas, would simply mean annexation pure and simple.

The learned Barrister went on to assert that:

If the expression "Southern Cameroons" has exposed us to any annexationist ambitions, then we will henceforth call ourselves AMBAZONIA.[6]

And so just like that the name "Ambazonia" became part of the lexicon of Anglophone Cameroon's struggle for self-determination.

This is what has come to be known as the "Southern Cameroons Question". Over the years the Central Government has shown a persistent unwillingness and inability to address these two key grievances of its Anglophone minority, rather preferring a brutal crackdown of its proponents. After decades of trying without success to peacefully draw attention to their grievances, a faction of Anglophone nationalists finally took up arms in 2017 to demand separation.

Growing Internal Fissures and Irresponsive Leadership

Derogatory expressions like *"pays organisateur"*, *"anti-sadinards"*, *"anti-tonti-nards"*, *"milice beti-bulu"*, *"les moutons"*, *"les bamendas'* etc., have become engraved in our national vocabulary. Banal as these expressions may seem, they are the outward manifestations of the deep-rooted socio-political cleavages that have become the hallmarks of the Cameroon society. They are profoundly divisive and, most unfortunately, often promoted and tolerated by political leaders from both sides of the political divide and buoyed by a pervasive clan mentality. In cyberspace and in the streets of the capitals of western countries, the so-called *"Brigade Anti Sadinards"* and the so-called *"Brigade Anti Tontinards"* - two groups with distinct ethnic identities and political affiliation - are in permanent confrontation with each other.

When faced with the great issues of the day, issues that can have a lasting impact on the fate of the country, Cameroonians have been quick to recoil to their ethnic affinities. In those instances, Cameroon as a cohesive nation-state simply ceases to exist and ethno-regional interests trump over national interests. So quite palpably, national unity and national integration as pillars of nation building do not seem to have worked. They have remained mere slogans. The New Deal turned out to be a Raw Deal and national development seems to

---

6   Dinka, G. (1985). *The New Social Order*. Yaounde. p. 8.

be in a logjam. The country is far more divided and less inclusive today than it was in 1961.

This sordid and inauspicious situation in which the country finds itself has been further exacerbated by failure of political leadership at all levels of the Cameroon society. Our leaders had fallaciously believed that unity and inclusiveness could be decreed or coerced. They failed to realize that it takes time, sustained effort and commitment to create a sense of commonality and trust among the diverse groups that make up the nation. Above all else, it demands a good example at the topmost echelons of the state.

Leadership failure and lack of vision have resulted in profound structural problems such as deepening poverty, high levels of youth under-employment and the inability to achieve the objectives and outcomes set out in different national development programs. Consequently, health and education standards are inadequate, critical infrastructure is dwindling relative to population growth, public and individual freedoms are daily being curtailed, the rule of law is being undermined, the democratic space is shrinking by the day and the state has become more and more oppressive, intolerant and authoritarian.

In addition, the decentralization process has proved insufficient and corruption has become rampant and pervasive. As a result, government has shown itself as incapable of delivering the most basic of services to its population. A case in point is potable water supply. Even though nearly all of Cameroon's 58 administrative divisions are named after great rivers, lakes and waterfalls, there is hardly any city or town in Cameroon, including its national and economic capitals, which can boast of a regular supply of clean and safe drinking water, six decades after unification.

At different times Mr. Biya himself has identified inertia, bureaucratic bottlenecks and corruption as the evil triad of the Cameroon public administration system. The problem with President Biya is that he often speaks of Cameroon's problems as if he is an outside consultant, hired to make an analysis of his country's ills. Listening to the man speak, you will never know that he is the lone individual in the country with the power, the authority and the responsibility to right the wrongs he is so adept at identifying.

Conclusion: Scope of Work and Summary of Chapters

Quite clearly all is not well with Cameroon. The country is a swirling vortex of atrophy in urgent need of redemption and renewal.

After sixty years of the Cameroonian experiment in nationhood and self-government, it has become obvious that the highly centralized, authoritarian Jacobin state model that French Cameroon inherited from France on 1 January 1960 and into which Southern (Anglophone) Cameroonians found themselves after 20 May 1972 has been nothing short of an unmitigated disaster. It has simply not worked. And since new results can never be obtained with old methods, there is therefore the urgent need to re-think, to re-engineer and to re-structure this nation from the bottom up, but with a renewed commitment to the promises that informed its founding and defined its post-unification aspirations. This is my case for the Refoundation of the Cameroon Nation. And this is the core objective of this book.

This book is essentially a political treatise, written with the main goal of eliciting an informed discussion on the state of the Cameroon nation, six decades after unification. It is a call for profound introspection and stock-taking of our achievements and our failures as a nation for the past sixty years. That is why in Chapter Two, I use internationally recognized performance appraisal indexes, evaluation reports of international lending institutions as well as the Cameroon Government's own assessment reports, as baselines for establishing the state of play. And by "state of play" I mean an appraisal of where we are as a nation, in terms of progress made, or lack thereof, in critical areas of our national life, such as the economy, education, health, poverty alleviation, reducing inequality, governance, civil and individual liberties and infrastructure. The starting point of this appraisal are the objectives set out in the different development policy frameworks and programs implemented during the course of the past thirty years, notably, the structural adjustment plans, the Poverty Reduction Programs and the two implementation frameworks of Cameroon Vision 2035, to wit, the Growth and Employment Strategy Paper and the National Development Strategy 2030. In order to make a credible assessment, I pored through, and exploited, thousands of pages of quantitative data from a myriad of sources. But because this book is clearly not intended as an academic work, I have intentionally decided not to load the reader with quantitative information such as graphs, diagrams and tables. Rather, I chose to summarize for the reader's benefit, the key findings of the data and the story they tell. I have endeavored to keep the narrative simple, less technical and more conversational so as to make it more accessible to a diverse readership.

This treatise is not only about diagnosing the nation's ills or showcasing its weaknesses. I also offer what I consider to be common sense solutions to some of the nation's teething problems. The solutions I offer are three-throng, over-arching, and governance-based, and are contained in Chapters Three, Four and Five. They are intended to serve as viable building blocks for the renewal of the promises, and the refounding of this nation. In this regard, in Chapter Three, I take a critical look at Cameroon's decentralization endeavors since independence and draw the conclusion that none of the decentralization frameworks developed and implemented since unification have proven adequate in resolving the nation's decentralized governance conundrum. And the reason for it is three-fold. First, there is the obvious lack of political will to pursue genuine decentralization; second, the country's ruling elite have an innate desire to hold on to centralized authority at all cost; and third, there is the recurrent fear of the nation's rulers that greater regional autonomy could elicit an appetite for secession. I note that twice in the last thirty years, the ruling elite has offered decentralization and even a "special status" as some sort of a peace offering to Anglophone Cameroonians. Yet, this has done precious little nothing to resolve both the Anglophone Problem and the Southern Cameroons Question I alluded to earlier in this chapter. Anglophone Cameroon nationalism is as strong as ever, and years of neglect has led to some factions of a separatist movement taking up arms to demand outright secession. And it can be reasonably assumed that some other regions may be tempted to do same, if their deeply rooted grievances, which are mostly governance-related and linked to service delivery, are not adequately addressed.

In this regard I propose a decentralized governance framework which involves the setting up of regional executive councils (headed by governors elected by direct suffrage) and regional legislative assemblies also elected by direct suffrage, both exercising a wide range of executive and legislative functions devolved to them through a Schedule of the Constitution. Such a framework, I argue, is a better reflection of the Principal-Agent paradigm of political leadership and agency. Moreso, it is more consistent with the principles of the inalienable right of a people to freely govern themselves. Ideally, such a framework should result in a re-distribution of power such that the people are put back at the center of the decision-making process. It should also allow for enhanced political accountability and a more efficient way of allocating and managing the nation's resources for development.

However, untangling the decentralization conundrum in itself is not enough. It should be accompanied by profound reforms in public service delivery. Any organization that fails to regularly innovate easily slumps into routine and redundancy. In that regard, in Chapter Four, I challenge Cameroon public affairs managers to draw inspiration from the concepts of New Public Management and Reinventing Government and develop a stronger framework for service delivery that is expeditious, efficient, effective and economical. In my proposed public service delivery model, I argue for a re-definition of the roles between the Central Government and the Regional Authorities, whereby the Central Government shall assume the role of an "enabling bystander" while the Regional Authorities take on a more operational or "doing" role.

In Chapter Five, I theorize that the renewal of the promises and the refounding of this nation, shall also depend on a large part on the quality of its political leadership. Since unification, I aver, Cameroon's rulers have practiced a top-down transactional leadership model that has now proven itself to be antiquated and unresponsive. I decry the National Assembly's unwillingness to show institutional leadership at the outset of the Anglophone Crisis in 2016. I note that going forward, the nation's rulers must embrace bargaining, negotiation, persuasion, and dialogue as critical leadership tools, especially when trying to resolve a conflict that can make or mar the nation. For, to bargain, to negotiate, to seek to persuade and to dialogue with citizens holding a viewpoint contrary to that of the government's is a not a sign weakness. Rather, it shows genuine leadership and a willingness to place the interest and the wellbeing of the nation above all other considerations. Drawing from the example of the leadership style of the rulers of Dubai and the founding President of Botswana I assert that to move this nation forward shall require a new political leadership paradigm – one that is bold, audacious, assertive but above all else, transformational in character; a leadership model that places the wellbeing of the citizenry at the center of all leadership endeavors.

This, in summary, is my three-prong overarching praxis for the refoundation of the Cameroon Nation and for the renewal of its foundational promises: untangling the decentralization conundrum, addressing the imperative of public service reform and envisioning a new political leadership paradigm.

Chapter Two

The State of Play

The Refoundation of the Cameroonian nation begins with an appraisal of the state of play. It is important to know where we are, otherwise, we cannot know where we are going, or where we ought to be. In this chapter, I shall attempt a comprehensive baseline analysis of some of the key sectors of our national life, namely:
* The Economy
* Human and Social Development (education, health, unemployment, inequality and poverty reduction)
* Governance and Institutional Capacity
* Infrastructure (roads and energy)
* Democracy, Civil and Individual Liberties.

I shall as much as possible, benchmark Cameroon's performance relative to other African countries of the same stature so as to show Cameroon's progress, or lack thereof, vis-à-vis these countries. My frames of reference are the various strategic frameworks and policy documents that, over the course of the last three decades, have been crafted and implemented in an attempt to put the economy back on track by enhancing growth and increasing the pace of socio-economic development. These include:
* The Five-year development plans
* The Structural Adjustment Plans
* The Enhanced Structural Adjustment Facility
* The different Poverty Reduction Strategy Papers
* Cameroon Vision 2035
* The Growth and Employment Strategy Paper
* The National Development Strategy 2030

I shall also link this attempt to the Government of Cameroon's efforts to meet its commitments under the Millennium Development Goals (MDGs) as well as the Sustainable Development Goals (SDGs).

Economic Growth and Development Trends

According to the World Bank, Cameroon is ranked as a lower middle-income economy. In the early 1960s, Cameroon, together with other newly independent Sub-Saharan Countries like Ghana and Cote d'Ivoire, was said to have better economic growth indicators than some Asian countries including some of those that came to be known as the "East Asian Tigers".

Under President Ahmadou Ahidjo's authoritarian one-party regime, the country enjoyed relative political stability for two decades (1961 to 1982). At unification in 1961, Cameroon practiced a mixed economic system in which private enterprise combined with centralized economic planning and government regulation. This economic policy was dubbed "Planned Liberalism". Agriculture remained the mainstay of the economy, in spite of the benefits of oil and mineral exploitation. The five-year development planning cycle implemented within a context of limited corruption, minimal waste in public spending and relatively high levels of macro-economic and monetary stability ensured that for a quarter of a century (1961 to 1985) after independence, Cameroon was on course to becoming one of the most prosperous nations in Africa.[1]

The Beginning of Economic Decline

This period of relative economic prosperity came to an end in 1985 when Cameroon was hit by an unprecedented economic crisis. In June 1987, President Paul Biya went before the National Assembly to publicly acknowledge the economic crisis for the first time. This came as a shock to Cameroonians because barely a year earlier, the President had assured the nation that the economy was doing great. The President blamed the economic crisis on the global economic downturn, characterized by falling commodity prices and trade deficits. However, many were also quick to point to the wasteful public spending and the barefaced corruption that were becoming endemic, barely five years into Mr. Biya's reign, as the main cause of the economic crisis. The causes notwithstanding, the President went on to announce to a befuddled nation the measures his government was taking to stem the crisis. He asked his compatriots to tighten their belts and

---

1   Tambi, M. D. (2015). Economic Growth, Crisis, and Recovery in Cameroon: A Literature Review. *Journal of Industrial Distribution & Business*, 6(1), 5-15.

roll up their shirt sleeves as difficult days lay head. The President warned that the State shall no longer be a milking cow. The following year, an IMF/World Bank-approved Structural Adjustment Program (SAP) was enacted to try and put the economy back on track. As with all IMF/World Bank supported, and Washington-Consensus-inspired SAPs, the measures included a cut in public spending, fiscal discipline, and privatization of state-owned enterprises and liberalization of the economy. However, the economy never fully recovered, leading to what economists have referred to as Cameroon's Lost Decade of the mid-80s to the mid-90s.

GDP Performance

Gross domestic product (GDP) - defined as the aggregate value of all services and goods produced within a country in any given year - is an important indicator of a country's economic power. The economic growth rate, expressed as a percentage, measures changes or growth in the economy (GDP) from year to year.

Statistically, Cameroon's GDP rose steadily since 2000, but not at a rate that allowed it to meet its strategic development goals of curbing poverty, inequality and underemployment. In 2000, Cameroon's GDP was estimated at USD 9.8 billion. This figure more than doubled in 2010 (USD 26.19 billion). Cameroon's GDP was estimated at USD 39.04 billion in 2020.[2] As commendable as this might seem, Cameroon's economic performance is far below a comparable country like Cote d'Ivoire (which is gradually coming out of a ten-year armed conflict) whose 2020 GDP was estimated at USD 61.5 billion and projected to reach USD 71.53 billion in 2021. Within the same period (2000 to 2020) Cameroon's economic growth rate averaged between 3 to 5 per cent. According to a 2018 World Bank report, over the last decade *"…the pace of economic growth has been too slow to lead to economic development".[3]* In fact, another World Bank report of 2010 had warned that *"Cameroon's growth achievement is disappointing and the country is not likely to meet most of the Millennium Development Goals (MDGs) on its current trajectory".[4]* This dismal economic performance has been further compounded by pervasive corruption and an unfavorable business environment not conducive for foreign and domestic investment

---

2   https://www.statista.com/statistics/446648/gross-domestic-product-gdp-in-cameroon
3   World Bank, Cameroon Education Reform Project, February 2018, p.2
4   World Bank: Cameroon, Fiscal Space for Growth and Development, September 2010, p. VIII.

Endemic Corruption and Poor Business Climate

In 1998 and again in 1999 Transparency International classified Cameroon as the most corrupt country in the world. Even though statistically, Cameroon's corruption index has improved over the years, corruption remains endemic. It is fair to surmise that Cameroon's corruption index looked better only because those of other countries became worse. Over the last 10 years, Cameroon averages as the 13th most corrupt country in Africa. This effectively means that Cameroon is within the top 20 per cent of most corrupt countries in Africa. For perspective, other countries within that bracket include weak, failing and conflict-ridden states like Somalia, South Sudan, D.R Congo, Burundi, Central Africa Republic, Chad, Guinea Bissau and Zimbabwe.

The pace of economic growth and development can be hastened by a business environment conducive for international and domestic investment. This is what the World Bank calls the Ease of Doing Business. The World Bank's Ease of Doing Business index measures a country's level of regulatory performance whereby changes over time reflect change in the economy's regulatory environment. The index is measured on a scale of 0 (lowest performance) to 100 (highest performance). The macro-areas which are covered are: starting a business, dealing with construction permits, getting electricity, registering property, getting credit, protecting minority investors, paying taxes, trading across borders, enforcing contracts, resolving insolvency, employing workers, and contracting with the government.[5]

Cameroon's performance in this area has been less than impressive. Between 2015 and 2020, Cameroon's score averaged 43, significantly below the average scores of countries like Ghana, Côte d'Ivoire, Kenya and Rwanda which were averaging between 50 and 80. In terms of rankings, Cameroon's position averages 165.92 out of 190 economies between 2009 and 2019, placing her within the bottom 15 per cent globally. However, since 2015, the World Bank Doing Business index has noted some attempts on the part of the Cameroon Government to improve its performance in the following categories:

* Getting Credit
* Starting a Business
* Enforcing Contracts
* Obtaining Construction Permits
* Getting Electricity
* Registering Property

---

5   https://www.doingbusiness.org/en/data/exploreeconomies/cameroon

* Resolving Insolvency
* Protecting Minority Investors

Human and Social Development

The level of human and social development of a country is measured in terms of continuous improvements in education, health, poverty alleviation, access to basic services like safe drinking water and electricity etc. In that regard, the UNDP's Human Development Index (HDI) is a quantitative measure of average achievement in these key dimensions of human development, often summarized as a long and healthy life, being knowledgeable and having a decent standard of living.

Cameroon has recorded significant progress in its human and social development efforts. Between 1990 and 2019, its overall HDI value increased from 0.448 to 0.563 (or an increase of 25.7 per cent), positioning Cameroon at 153 out of 189 countries and territories. More specifically, Cameroon's life expectancy at birth increased by 5.9 years, mean years of schooling increased by 2.8 years and expected years of schooling increased by 4.1 years. Cameroon's GNI per capita increased by about 15.5 percent between 1990 and 2019.[6] However, the 2020 UNDP Human Development Report noted that:

> Cameroon's 2019 HDI of 0.563 is below the average of 0.631 for countries in the medium human development group and above the average of 0.547 for countries in Sub-Saharan Africa. From Sub Saharan Africa, Cameroon is compared with Ghana and Madagascar, which have HDIs ranked 138 and 164, respectively.[7]

However, the HDI does not tell the whole story. A careful analysis shows that Cameroon is still lagging behind in most of the key human and social development sectors like education, health, poverty alleviation and inequality. Take education, for instance.

The Challenge of Attaining Universal Primary Education

In his traditional Youth Day Message of 10 February 2000, President Biya declared free primary education in public schools. His declaration was an affirmation of the right to education enshrined in the Constitution of the Republic

---

6   See the 2020 UNDP Human Development Report, p. 2
7   Ibid, p. 4

of Cameroon which states unequivocally that *"The State shall guarantee the child's right to education. Primary education shall be compulsory"*.[8] The President's declaration was also intended to emphasize the country's commitment to meet the Millennium Development Goal of attaining universal primary education by 2015.

The government has made commendable progress in terms of the increase in the number of schools created and built. School enrolment numbers have also been steadily rising. There has been significant increase in the recruitment and deployment of teachers. However, these significant achievements notwithstanding, the strategic goal of attaining universal primary education was not reached in 2015, and definitely not in 2020. The reasons for this are manifold, some of which include, stagnating Primary Completion Rate numbers, insufficient mastery of basic language and mathematics competency by the learners and the paucity of skilled teachers, especially in mathematics.

The Primary Completion Rate (PCR) is the percentage of pupils completing the last year of primary school. It is calculated by taking the total number of pupils in the last grade of primary school, minus the number of repeaters in that grade, divided by the total number of children of official graduation age. A rising PCR is therefore one of the key indicators of progress towards the attainment of Universal Primary Education. According to the score card for primary education cited in the World Bank's 2018 "Cameroon Education Reform Project", between 2013/14 and 2014/15, the Primary Completion Rate plateaued with a light increase of two percentage points (from 74.5 per cent to 76.3 per cent). Data from the Global Partnership for Education (GPE) show that between 2015/16 and 2017/18, overall PCR dropped by nearly 10 percentage points (from 74.2 per cent to 64.5 per cent), with a 9-percentage point drop with respect to girls.[9] In 2019, Cameroon's PCR rose by a percentage point (65.5 per cent total with 62 per cent in respect to girls). This performance is well below that of comparable countries like Cote d'Ivoire (78.6 per cent), Rwanda (97 per cent) but above Senegal (61 per cent) and Burkina Faso (59 per cent).[10] At this pace, the World Bank concluded, *"it is unlikely that the target of the Education Sector Strategy…of 100% [Primary Completion Rate] shall be reached in 2020".*[11] And of course it wasn't. It is however, important to note that in the five years prior to 2015, Cameroon was making considerable progress in its PCR. The drop can be attributed to the Boko Haram conflict in the Northern regions and the

---

8   Preamble of the 1996 Constitution of the Republic of Cameroon.
9   https://www.globalpartnership.org/where-we-work/cameroon
10   https://data.worldbank.org/indicator/SE.PRM.CMPT.ZS
11   The World Bank Cameroon Education Reform Project, February 2018, p. 5.

armed conflict in the Anglophone regions, both of which are directly targeting the education sector.

Apart from a declining PCR, there are also wide imbalances in school attendance based on gender, regional and socio-economic characteristics. Net attendance for girls in rural areas is only 65 per cent, compared to 78 per cent for boys in rural areas. Enrollment of boys exceed that among girls (139 per cent compared to 129 per cent in 2014/15 respectively). Between 2011– 2014 only 69 per cent of both boys and girls made the transition from primary school to secondary school.

Furthermore, the quality of primary/basic education is described as poor and often characterized by low achievement at primary level. According to the 2014 PASEC assessments[12], less than 30 per cent of pupils (29.7 per cent) were deemed to have "sufficient" language competency at the beginning of the primary education cycle. However, a higher percentage of pupils (55.3) met the "sufficient" threshold in mathematics at the beginning of the primary education cycle. Still according to PASEC assessments for 2014, less than half (48.8 per cent) of the number of pupils graduating from primary school were assessed as having "sufficient" language competency. That figure is down to 35.5 per cent with regard to mathematics. The second PASEC evaluation carried out in 2019 showed no improvement as only 32.9 per cent of pupils graduating from primary school were assessed to have sufficient language competency, compared to 48.9 per cent in 2014. The mathematics competence however, rose from 35.5 percent in 2014 to 58.4 per cent in 2019.

This trend is largely consistent with a 2016 assessment carried out by the Cameroon Government through its Unité d'Acquis Scolaire (UAS) or School Achievement Unit. The assessment measured the thresholds for the mastery of basic literacy and numeracy skills of learners in classes 2, 4 and 6 of the primary cycle of both the Anglophone and Francophone Sub-systems of education. According to the evaluation, overall, 68.2 per cent of pupils graduating from primary school during the 2015-2016 academic year were assessed as having "difficulties" mastering basic mathematical operations. In fact, 90.4 per cent of pupils were assessed as having difficulties in the "solving problems" sub-category. For the same year, and still according to the evaluation, the percentage of

---

12   Program d'Analyse des Systèmes Éducatifs de la CONFEMEN (PASEC) is an assessment framework developed by the Conference of Ministers of Education in Sub Saharan Francophone Countries (CONFEMEN). It measures basic language and mathematics competences for learners at the beginning and at the end of the primary education cycle in some 14 Francophone countries in Sub Saharan Africa.

pupils deemed to have acquired the expected language competence at gradua-tion was 49.7. About 50 per cent of the pupils were assessed as having acquired the requisite skills in the "reading and comprehension of text" category, the best performance in all six categories that were measured under "language of instruction".[13]

With regard to the competency of teachers, PASEC 2019 assessed that 72.3 per cent of primary school teachers in Cameroon displayed a high level of language competency (comprehension and writing). This performance is lower than in comparable countries like Gabon (74.2 per cent), Benin and Burkina Faso (75 per cent), Senegal (81.9 per cent) and Cote d'Ivoire (87.8 per cent). Only 37 per cent of Cameroon's primary school teachers were deemed to have "sufficient" competency in mathematics. This is well below the performance of other countries like Benin (60.5 per cent) Cote d'Ivoire (52.6 per cent) Senegal (52.2 per cent) and Togo (54.2 per cent).

Both the UAS and PASEC assessments showed that pupils in public schools and rural schools perform worse than students in private and urban schools.[14] Also, pupils with textbooks tend to perform better than those without textbooks. The PASEC assessments for both 2014 and 2019 also noted that repeaters and older students do not necessarily perform better, and girls perform less than the boys with regard to mathematics. Overall, the 2019 PASEC assessment noted that 60.6 per cent of Cameroon's primary school learners did not have the requisite competency in language and mathematics that can allow them to continue their studies without struggling.

Secondary Education: Ballooning Enrolments but Inadequate Infrastructure

The past forty years have seen a significant increase in the number of gov-ernment secondary schools (both first cycle and second cycle grammar and technical) created and built. During the first two decades after unification in 1961 in the North West Province, for instance, there were only five government secondary schools, namely, Cameroon College of Arts, Science and Technology (CCAST) Bambili, Government Bilingual High School Bamenda, Government High School Mbengwi, Government High School Nkambe and Government High School Wum. The lone Government Technical High School in Bamenda was also built in the mid-eighties. The same level of expansion of access to public secondary schools can be seen in all the regions. Today, virtually every hamlet

---

13   Enquete UAS2016, "Rapport de l'Evaluation des Acquis des Eleves CP/CL2, CE2/CL4 ET CM2/CL6 en Langue d'enseignement et Mathematiques", 2017. p. 17.
14   The World Bank Cameroon Education Reform Project, February 2018, pp. 5-7

in Cameroon has a government secondary/high school.

However, like in the primary education sector, secondary education is plagued by insufficient learning outcomes due to problems of inadequate infrastructure relative to levels of enrolment, poor curriculum, lack of textbooks and other didactic materials and paucity of trained teachers. In 2016 slightly less than half (51 per cent) of teachers in lower secondary schools were trained. In addition, the technical/vocational secondary schools suffer from poorly equipped or antiquated workshops (where they do exist) for practical work. For instance, when I visited the motor mechanics workshop of the Government Technical High School (GTHS) Bamenda in 2014, I discovered that they were using the engine block of a 40-year-old Renault 4 to teach the students the basic mechanical features of a vehicle engine. This was happening in an age of highly computerized automobiles. Besides, the only person I know who still drives a Renault 4 is Pope Francis. I strongly doubt that any of the kids being trained at GTHS Bamenda shall ever get the chance to repair the Holy Father's Renault 4. So, for whom and for what market are they being trained?

However, the Global Partnership for Education noted some significant improvements in the lower secondary school cycle. These include an improvement in student-trained teacher ratio from 60 in 2011 down to 47 in 2014 and a six-percentage point increase in completion rates from 40.9 in 2012 to 46.6 in 2015.

According to a World Bank assessment, factors that contribute to these inadequate learning outcomes include, shortage of teachers and a teacher training program that is too theoretical without special focus on practical experience; lack of textbooks, teaching and learning material; very few early childhood development programs; weak sector management and governance (marked by a lack of an accountability and M&E framework). There are four ministries responsible for education and a fifth responsible for youth affairs and youth policy. This, according to a 2017 GPE assessment, has led to lack of cohesion in the sector. The last and by no means the least is the issue of financing. The GPE and the World Bank assess that despite recent efforts to improve on budget allocation, financing remains inadequate to meet the needs of education sector. In 2016, the World Bank reports, the GDP per capita allocation for education in Cameroon was about 3.2 per cent, lower than in comparable countries in Africa and around the world. The budget allocated to the education sector represented an average of 14.2 per cent of total public expenditure executed annually between 2010 and 2016, which is still 6 percentage points short of the GPE's recommended benchmark of 20 per cent.[15]

Higher Education: Not suited for Purpose

The aims and purpose of higher education have changed considerably in the course of the last five centuries. For instance, when the Puritans founded Harvard College in 1636, the purpose of higher education then was to produce "a learned clergy and a lettered people" and "to develop learners to work towards improving the conditions of society at large".[16] The early institutions of higher learning were created by faith-based organizations. So, quite understandably, they had a spiritual and vocational twist. Harvard, Dartmouth and Yale, for example, were all founded by Congregationalists with the aim of preparing men for the Christian ministry or clergymen for civil service in the Anglican Church. By the 18th and 19th centuries the purpose of university studies had evolved to include the education of an elite group of young men for the learned professions and for positions of leadership in society.

Soon after gaining independence, most African countries like Cameroon were immediately faced with the problem of the lack of trained manpower to lead and to govern the new nations. So, like in Europe and America in the 17th and 18th centuries the first universities were created essentially to produce young men and women with the required technocratic and leadership skills needed to jump-start socio-economic development. Cameroon's first ever institution of higher education, the Federal University of Yaoundé, was created in 1962, just one year after unification. The immediate purpose of the university was to train a high level, skilled workforce to replace the departing colonial admin-istrators. There are currently eight state-owned universities, a good number of undergraduate and post-graduate level professional training schools as well as many other private institutions of higher learning offering a myriad of courses.

Even though it can be argued that the increase in universities and other insti-tutions of higher learning in Cameroon has improved access to higher education, this increase in enrolment numbers has not been matched by a corresponding increase in infrastructure nor has it led to improvements in the quality of learn-ing. A study of Cameroon's public universities carried out by researchers of the Institute of International and Comparative Education of the Zhejiang Normal University and published in 2019, showed that state university programs were

---

15   Idem p.8.

16   Chan, R.Y. (2016). Understanding the Purpose of Higher Education: An Analysis of the Economic and Social Benefits for Completing a College Degree: *JEPPA*, Volume 6, Issue 5, p. 6.

mostly based on the social sciences and the humanities that had little impact on economic growth. Pushing the argument further, the researchers averred that:

> In 2010, the faculties of law and social sciences alone enroll 70% of the total tertiary enrolment while the engineering programmes (which is supposed to train students for infrastructure projects in accordance with the country's objectives for construction) and agriculture programmes (which is the main source of growth and livelihood of the population) count for only 5% and less than 0.4% respectively. A general observation shows that almost all universities present the same programmes with a strong emphasis placed on social sciences and humanities.[17]

A 1993 university reform sought to correct exactly these kinds of anomalies. One of the stated goals of the reform was to make university programs more professional and more responsive to the exigencies and demands of a fast-evolving labor market. However, to date no significant progress has been made in that regard. Cameroonian institutions of higher learning are still chronically lagging behind in the development of Science, Technology, Engineering, and Mathematics (STEM) curriculum.

Apart from the problem of soaring enrollment rates unmatched by an increase in infrastructure, other problems plaguing higher education on Cameroon include:

* Inadequate numbers of teachers leading to a high lecturer-student ratio
* Lack of funding (80 per cent of the budget of state universities come from state subsidies which are irregular and undependable).
* Limited opportunities and grants for research.

With a curriculum tilted more towards the liberal arts, and with fast declining quality of learning, the higher education system in Cameroon is mainly producing certificate holders with no marketable skills. No wonder a majority of its graduates are jobless and the nation lacks locally-trained skilled workforce needed to implement its social and economic transformational agenda. In short, it is a system no longer fit for purpose.

---

17 Guiake, M., & Tianzue, Z. (2019). Higher Education's Curriculum and Challenges of the 21st Century: The Case Study of Cameroonian Public Universities. *Journal of Education and Practice*, *10*(18), p. 123.

The Health Sector: Poor and Inadequate

The health sector has not fared any better. A 2016 "Health Analytical Profile" for Cameroon, co-authored by the Cameroon Ministry of Health and the World Health Organization concluded that *"…the health system performance is poor and inadequate."*[18] And it is not difficult to fathom why.

There are approximately 1.1 physicians and 7.8 nurses and midwives per 10,000 population.[19] This falls far short of the WHO recommended ratio of 2.5 medical staff (physicians, nurses and midwives) per 1,000 people needed to provide adequate coverage with primary care interventions.[20] Even then, the medical staff are inequitably distributed between urban and rural areas, and between regions. The cities of Douala and Yaoundé host the bulk of health facilities and medical personnel, while the North, Adamaoua and South regions have the fewest health workers.[21]

In 2012, 70.42 per cent (474.5 billion CFA francs) of health expenditure was borne by households. This was the third highest in Sub Saharan Africa, where the average is 34 per cent. In addition, about 64 per cent of households cannot access healthcare because they perceive the cost of healthcare as high.[22] According to a situational analysis of the state of health risk protection in Cameroon done by Chenjoh Joseph Nde et al., and published in the 2019 edition of the Universal Journal of Public Health, only 6.46 per cent of Cameroonians are covered by a community health insurance scheme; by 2014 there were about 43 active mutual health organizations providing coverage for about 63,000 people or 0.2 per cent of the population with contributions ranging from 6 to 10 USD per person per year. Also, there were some 16 private health insurance companies in existence by 2014, providing coverage to approximately 190,406 persons with annual subscription rates ranging around 310 USD per adult and 150 USD per child. These relatively high rates, the authors claimed, means that poor people who need health insurance coverage the most are automatically excluded.[23]

As with the education sector, the health sector also suffers from inadequate

18 Health Analytical Profile 2016 Cameroon, p. x.
19 WHO Cameroon Fact Sheet, 2010; https://www.who.int/workforcealliance/countries/cmr/en/.
20 WHO, World Health Report 2006.
21 19 Ministry of Public Health Directorate of Health Resources (MINSANTE DRH), 2012; Cameroun : Analyse de la situation des ressources humaines pour la santé, 2010)
22 Nde, C. J., Raymond, A., Saidu, Y., Cheng, N. I., Nzuobontane, D., Atemnkeng, J. T., & Mbacham, W. F. (2019). Reaching universal health coverage by 2035: is Cameroon on track. *Universal Journal of Public Health*, 7(3), 110-117.
23 Ibid, p.111.

financing. In April 2001, African Union countries met in Abuja and pledged to set a target of allocating at least 15 per cent of their annual budget to improve the health sector. This is what is known as the Abuja Declaration. In Cameroon, the share of the health sector in total recurrent spending is estimated at about 8 percent,[24] almost 50 per cent below the Abuja Target. In its 10-year assessment of progress made by African governments towards attaining the Abuja Target, the WHO cited Cameroon as one of the 27 countries making "insufficient progress" in meeting its commitments under the Abuja Declaration. [25]

In order to address these shortcomings and gaps in the health sector, the Cameroon government has been trying to develop a Universal Health Care Coverage plan, as part of its commitment under the SDGs, and in a bid to achieve its strategic objective of attaining full universal health care coverage for the population by 2035. It is not known when the plan shall be rolled out.

Curbing Unemployment and Poverty

Over the years social science has firmly established a nexus between unemployment and poverty. An unemployed or an underemployed person lacks the income that can enable him or her fulfill his or her most basic needs like health, food, shelter, clothing and education. In that regard the individual is thus deprived of his or her right to a decent living. Reducing poverty and unemployment is also inextricably linked to the pace of economic growth. These dynamics are aptly captured in Cameroon's Vision 2035 program and its first implementation framework, the Growth and Employment Strategy Paper (GESP).

The Strategic Goals of Cameroon Vision 2035 and the GESP

The "Cameroon Vision 2035 Working Paper" of February 2009 affirmed that:

> Poverty alleviation implies bringing poverty to minimal levels that can be tolerated at the social level notably by ensuring strong, sustained and job-generating growth on the one hand and by increasing, extending and improving social services, including health, education, housing, training, water, electricity, roads, etc. on the other hand. The status of middle income country will concretize the objective of doubling at least the average income to ensure that Cameroon progresses from a low income to a middle income country by enhancing growth to a two-digit level

24 The World Bank, "Cameroon Fiscal Policy for Growth and Development", September 2010, p. X
25 WHO, 'The Abuja Declaration: Ten Years On", p.2.

by 2017 and maintaining this level for a number of years.[26]

The GESP, which was drafted to serve as the main implementation framework of the first ten years (2010-2020) of Cameroon Vision 2023 re-echoed the same priorities:

> The GESP which will cover the first ten years of the long-term development vision will focus on accelerating growth, creating formal employment and reducing poverty, consequently, it aims to (i) increase the average annual growth rate to 5.5 per cent over the period 2010-2020; (ii) reduce the underemployment rate from 75.8 per cent to less than 50 per cent in 2020 with the creation of tens of thousands of formal positions per annum over the next ten years; (iii) reducing the income poverty rate from 39.9 per cent in 2007 to 28.7 per cent in 2020.[27]

Unfortunately, none of these lofty objectives were attained.

Double digit growth was never achieved in 2017. Between 2009 and 2019, Cameroon's economy grew at an annual average of about 3-5 per cent, and contracted even further (2.4 per cent) in 2020, according to the African Development Bank.[28] The unemployment rate has also plateaued at about 3.5 per cent; this figure is up to 6 per cent with regard to youth unemployment, according to ILO data. While this is still a commendable improvement from 1999/2000 when unemployment rate was as high as 8.12 per cent, the teething problem of under-employment remains unresolved. Under-employment - defined as the share of workers earning less than about US$2 a day or working less than 35 hours a week, while willing to work more – was estimated at 75 per cent in 2010 and largely remained unchanged in 2020 (the completion point of the GESP).

The Poverty Rate

Statistical progress, or lack thereof, in a country's efforts to reduce poverty is measured through the poverty rate. The national poverty rate is the percentage of the population living below the national poverty line as reflected in household surveys. In 2014, poverty rate at the national poverty line for Cameroon stood at 37.5 per cent, a significant reduction from 53.3 percent in 1996. However, with about 10 million people (out of a population of 26 million) still living below

---

26   Cameroon Vision 2035 Working Paper, p.vii
27   GESP, P.17
28   According to Statista.com, GDP growth rate for Cameroon in 2020 is -2.77.

the poverty line, more than 70 percent of the population paying for their own health care needs, a Gini Coefficient of 46.6 which ranks Cameroon among the top 16 percent of the world's most unequal countries in terms of income distribution, and poor educational outcomes, Cameroon can hardly be said to be making any progress towards increasing employment and reducing poverty and income inequality.

Governance, Civil Service Performance and Institutional Capacity

The Ibrahim Index of African Governance (IIAG) is one of the most authoritative and transparent tools that measures and monitors governance performance on the continent. The Mo Ibrahim Foundation, authors of the IIAG, defines governance as *"the provision of the political, social and economic public goods and services that every citizen has the right to expect from their state, and that a state has the responsibility to deliver to its citizens."* In this regard, the IIAG measures and monitors a country's governance performance across four key categories seen as key indicators of a government's capacity to deliver key public services and perform the core functions of a state. These four categories are i) Safety and the Rule of law. ii) Participation and Human Rights. iii) Sustainable Economic Opportunity. iv) Human Development.[29]

Recent Cameroon Governance Assessment

In 2017 the overall governance score for all of Africa's 54 countries was 49.9/100, a trend classified as 'slowing improvement'. Within this context and for the same year, Cameroon had an overall governance score of 46.2/100, ranking 36 out of 54 countries, with a trend classified as *'increasing deterioration'*.[30] A closer examination of the IIAG categories and sub-categories shows why Cameroon's governance performance is seen as deteriorating. The category "Safety and Rule of Law" measures the extent to which governments deliver safety for citizens through assessing whether the state has the monopoly over violence, provides a safe and secure environment for the pursuit of individual or group endeavours, and guarantees personal security. The subcategory "Rule of Law" assesses the extent to which states have effective methods of resolving disputes and enforcing law through a judicial mechanism free of state control. "Transparency & Accountability" measures the degree to which public officials,

29   https://mo.ibrahim.foundation/iiag
30   Anti-corruption strategies for authoritarian States, Transparency International, CHR Michelsen Institute (2018) https://knowledgehub.transparency.org/helpdesk/anti-corruption-strategies-in-authoritarian-states.

institutions and the private sector are subject to oversight and scrutiny by other institutions and citizens, in order to make the government responsive in the pursuit of the public interest. Between 2013 and 2017, more than half of Africa's countries (28) managed to improve scores in the Safety and Rule of Law category. By contrast, Cameroon experienced the largest deterioration with an overall score of 40.3/100, which is -9.6 points lower than in 2008.

The "Participation and Human Rights" category measures civil and political rights and freedoms by assessing citizen participation in the political and electoral process, respect for basic rights, and the absence of gender discrimination through the sub-categories Participation, Rights and Gender. Between 2008 and 2017 the African average score for Participation & Human Rights increased significantly, averaging 49.2/100 in 2017. For that same year Cameroon scored 39/100 for this category, 10 points below the continental average. Cameroon, however, showed some slight improvement in the "Sustainable Economic Opportunity" category. This category measures the extent to which governments enable their citizens to pursue economic goals and provide the opportunity to prosper. The measured subcategories are Public Management and Business Environment, Infrastructure and the rural sector. In 2017 the continental average score was 44.8/100, only +0.1 points higher than 2008. Comparatively, Cameroon scored 47/100 in 2017, three points higher than the overall African average.

The "Human Development" category assesses whether governments provide poverty mitigation and alleviation, educational opportunities, health care, medical and sanitary services. These public goods are captured in the three sub-categories: welfare, education and health. This category continues to be Africa's best trending dimension. The continent's 2017 average score for this category was 52.8/100, +3.5 points higher than 2008. The IIAG assessed Cameroon's performance in this category to be commendable with a 58.2/100, close to 6 points above the continental average.

Over-Centralization and Diminished Civil Service Performance

In a general sense, it is a country's civil service that drives government performance. But a near Jacobin over-centralized governance model has effectively crippled civil service performance in Cameroon, making it unlikely for the country to attain the objectives set out in its development programs such as the NDS30 and Cameroon Vision 2035. A case in point is the over-centralization of the public investment budget, which has in turn led to the slow pace of the execution of projects needed to move the country forward. A 2010 World Bank evaluation report found that the central administration was responsible for the execution of more than 90 percent of the public investment budget, to the det-riment of local councils. As a result, only about 50 per cent of public investment budget was being executed. And even though the public investment allotment to the priority sectors like health and education has been considerably increased, the rate of execution of projects for these areas was around 22 per cent.

The same report described the Civil Service's ability to deliver crucial services as *"severely constrained"* due to *"...a shortage of qualified personnel in key sectors, lack of meritocracy or performance incentives, red tape in personnel administration, and ineffective disciplinary procedures [that]still undermine performance"*.[31]

With this kind of numbers and with this kind of institutional mindset, it is hard to imagine how the country can move ahead.

Multiplicity of Line Ministries with Conflicting Mandates

Cameroon's public sector performance has been further undermined by a relatively high number of line ministries. In some instances, the functions and responsibilities of line ministries compete and overlap with those of parastatal agencies and so-called permanent secretariats and commissions.

For most of the first two decades after unification in 1961, President Ahmadou Ahidjo maintained a lean cabinet averaging 20 line ministries and 25 ministers. For instance the first government of the unitary state formed in July 1972 was made up of 26 ministers and 18 ministerial departments. Under President Biya, the number of ministers and ministerial departments have almost tripled those under Ahmadou Ahidjo. The government of 4 January 2019 com-prises 38 line ministries (if you include the National Delegation for National Security) and 71 members of government (comprised of the Prime Minister, Ministers of State, Ministers, Minister Delegates, Secretaries of State). It is not unusual to see a line ministry, like the Ministry of Justice, headed by a Minister of State who is assisted by both a Minister-Delegate and a Secretary of State. With a population of 26 million and a GDP of 39 billion USD (in 2019), Cameroon's government can be considered heavy, especially when benchmarked to other countries with bigger populations and higher GDPs.

Take for instance, South Africa, Africa's second largest economy and Kenya, the East African Community's largest economy. With a population of almost 60 million and a GDP of 351 billion USD (2019), South Africa currently has 28 line ministries and 64 cabinet ministers. Kenya, with a population of 47 million and a GDP of 95.5 billion USD, has 21 members of government (or

---

31   The World Bank, "Cameroon: Fiscal Policy for Growth Development', September 2010, p.viii.

Cabinet Secretaries). In fact, the Kenyan Constitution allows for a maximum of 22 ministries.

As can be expected, the relatively high number of line ministries in Cameroon means there are over-lapping responsibilities between them, often with very little coordination. For instance, there are four ministries in charge of education and a fifth in charge of youth affairs. Responsibility for "local" and "rural" development is shared between the Ministry of Decentralization and Local Development and the Ministry of Agriculture and Rural Development. "Regional Planning" is the responsibility of quite another Ministry, namely, the Ministry of Economy, Planning and Regional Planning. The management of the public investment budget is a shared responsibility between the Ministries of Finance (formerly the Ministry of Economy and Finance) and the Ministry of Economy, Planning and Regional Planning (formerly the Ministry of Planning, Development Programming and Regional Planning).

In addition to line ministries, there are, in some cases, parastatal agencies and permanent secretariats and commissions exercising similar functions. For instance, there is a Ministry of Public Contracts which operates side by side with a Public Contracts Regulatory Agency. The Ministry of Decentralization exists analogously with the National Council on Decentralization. There is a Ministry of Public Service and Administrative Reform and there is a Permanent Secretariat for Administrative Reform described as a "technical organ" of the Ministry charged with assisting it in the accomplishment of its mission A Ministry of Youth Affairs was created in 2004. Five years later, in 2009, the Ministry created a Cameroon National Youth Council. The Council is said to be an apolitical, lay and non-profit making institution, placed under the supervision of the Minister of Youth Affairs. Even though the Council is officially said to be apolitical, it is the Minister (a political appointee) who organizes the election of its leaders and funds its activities. The multiplicity of government line ministries and the tangential increase in the number of members of government, especially after the return to multi-party politics in 1990, was never intended to improve public service delivery nor was it intended to enhance institutional capacity. Rather, the main goal was to compensate political allies and cronies of the regime.

Cameroon is essentially an autocracy where the president wields overwhelming executive power. The combination of over-centralization and a near imperial presidential system has resulted in the deliberate weakening of the capacity of the nation's institutions. In their pivotal book *Why Nations Fail*, Daron Acemoglu and James Robinson argue that it is the quality of its institutions that determine whether a nation is rich or poor, weak or strong. The authors make a difference between political and economic "inclusive institutions" and political and economic "extractive Institutions". Political institutions are said to be inclusive when they are sufficiently centralized and pluralistic. When either of these conditions are absent, they are said to be extractive. On their part, economic institutions are described as extractive when the resources of the nation are diverted to benefit a small ruling elite and inclusive when they are meant to promote broad-based socio-economic growth for the benefit of the masses. In this regard the authors aver that *"Nations fail when they have extractive economic institutions, supported by extractive political institutions that impede and even block economic growth"*.[32]

Even though Cameroon likes to pride itself as a pluralistic democracy, the fact of the matter is that all its institutions are placed under the strict control of the president and his allies. Both houses of parliament are dominated by the ruling party. The Minister of Justice (who is always an ally of the president) exercises complete control over the Judiciary. Heads of institutions meant to support democracy and the rule of law - like the National Human Rights Commission, the Elections Commission, the National Anti-Corruption Commission, and the National Communications Council – are appointed by presidential decree and function with very little parliamentary or civil society oversight.

Under such circumstances, it is hard to see institutions in Cameroon as independent, transparent and especially as inclusive. Rather, they are tailored to serve the needs of the presidency and to defend the interests of an entrenched political hegemony. This explains why ministerial departments and other public agencies are created, not to improve service delivery, promote broad-based socio-economic growth and development or enhance public sector performance but mostly as sinecures to compensate political allies and spread financial benefits to political allies.

Infrastructure Development

Without doubt it is the quality and quantity of a country's infrastructure that drives economic growth and enhances broad-based socio-economic development. The quality and quantity of transportation systems, communication networks, sewage, water, and electric systems are all examples of the kind of physical infrastructure that underpin a country's growth. This is because infrastructure increases efficiency, reduces production costs, thus creating incentives for international and domestic investment. That is why countries that have expressed the desire

---

32   Acemoglu, D., & Robinson, J. A. (2012). *Why Nations Fail: The Origins of Power, Prosperity and Poverty*. New York: Crown. p. 83.

to "emerge", pay a lot of attention to the development of critical infrastructure. It is no different with Cameroon.

The Growth and Employment Strategy Paper – 2010/2020 placed a high premium on infrastructure and assigned the task of improving the country's infrastructure to five ministerial departments, namely, the Ministries of Water and Energy, Public Works, Urban Development and Housing, Transport, Land Tenure and State Property and Posts and Telecommunications. The GESP affirmed that infrastructure is the pillar on which the development and competitiveness of the economy shall be built because *"It helps to cut the costs of production and transaction, facilitates the activity, increases the volume of production and spurs social progress".*[33]

In this regard the strategy defined some core objectives that were to be achieved through the implementation of 42 programs centered around maintenance, rehabilitation, extension/construction of the road network; railway, air transport, maritime transport infrastructure; posts and telecommunications infrastructure; urban housing and energy and hydraulic infrastructure; enhancing the performance of the construction industry, governance of infrastructure, the road works planning and programming system; ameliorating and facilitating access to telecoms/ICT services and improving land and State property management.[34]

It is not hard to fathom why the government is paying so much attention to infrastructure development. The past two decades have seen a steady degradation and dwindling of Cameroon's infrastructural fabric, especially its urban, road and energy networks.

Declining Infrastructural Fabric

In 1985, the municipality of Bamenda (Headquarters of the North West Region), with a population of about 200,000 at the time, could boast of an urban road network of about 50 km of paved roads. Electricity and water supply were fairly constant. Most of the town's infrastructure had been upgraded to host the Agro-pastoral Show and the National Congress of the ruling Cameroon National Union (CNU) party in 1985. Today, more than 30 years later, Bamenda's urban infrastructure has all but disappeared. The city of more than 500,000 inhabitants can hardly boast of 5kms of regularly maintained paved roads. Water shortages and electricity blackouts, hitherto unknown in the city, have now become common place. Something as essential and as basic as a waste collection and

33   GESP, p9.
34   Idem.

disposal system is nonexistent. As a result, Bamenda, which used to be one of the cleanest and healthiest cities in the country, is now nothing but one giant rubbish heap. In short, the quality and the quantity of the city's infrastructure has not been able to keep up with the demands of its burgeoning population. And the situation has gotten worse with the armed conflict raging in the region.

In 1992 I carried out some studies on the urban growth patterns of Bamenda municipality, as part of research work for an end of course dissertation submitted to the National School of Administration and Magistracy. In the study I predicted that in 25 years, Bamenda shall grow to become a giant metropolitan area, absorbing the nearby semi-urban municipalities of Bali, Bafut, Bambui/Bambili and Akum/Santa. I shared my findings with the then Government Delegate to the Bamenda City Council with the proposal that the Government needed to start thinking ahead by developing a master plan that took into consideration this projected urban growth trajectory. It is obvious my proposal was never given any serious thought.

There has been some commendable improvement in road infrastructure in the country in the past 20 years under the "Cameroon of Greater Ambitions", "Cameroon of Greater Achievements" and "Cameroon Vision 2035" programs. But unfortunately, the population growth rate has outpaced the rate of infrastructure development.

Sixty years after independence the country's national road network is antiquated, poor and inadequate.

Inadequate Road Network

In 2010, Cameroon was estimated to have about 50,000 km of roads of which about 5,000 km (or 10 per cent) were paved, placing Cameroon at the 78th position globally. In March 2018, Cameroon's Minister of Public Works informed that the linear density of the national road network was increasing at a satisfying pace. According to the Minister, between 2010 and 2016, this density increased from 5,240 km to 6,760 km, on a target of 9,558 km by 2020.[35] Sixty years after unification, Cameroon is still trying to construct its first expressway to link the political capital of Yaoundé and the economic capital of Douala. This modest progress notwithstanding, the country still lags behind in terms of the quality of its road infrastructure, compared to African countries of a similar stature.

Every year the World Economic Forum publishes The Road Quality

35   https://www.businessincameroon.com/transport/3003-7922

Indicator as one of the components of the Global Competitiveness Index. The indicator is an assessment of the quality of roads in a given country based on data from the WEF Executive Opinion Survey, among others. It measures the quality of roads on a scale of 1 (low) to 7 (high). Between 2006 and 2019, Cameroon's score averaged 2.58. And between 2010 and 2019 Cameroon was within the bottom ten of 38 Sub Saharan Africa countries that were polled. Other countries within that bracket include Chad, D.R Congo, Mozambique, Guinea, and Nigeria.[36]

Hydro Power Potentials and Access to Electricity

With regard to energy, according to the World Bank, Cameroon's hydro-power potentials are estimated at 12, 000 MW but only 721 MW have so far been developed in Edea, Song Loulou and Lagdo.[37] Access to electricity averages 48 per cent but very low (14 per cent) in rural areas. High power costs, the World Banks says, are a key impediment to competitiveness, growth and poverty reduction. As a result, the Bank estimates that lack of reliable electricity shall cost 5 per cent in lost enterprise revenues and 2 per cent in lost GDP growth p.a.[38]

In order to defray this energy deficit, the Lom Pangar Hydropower Project was launched as a priority infrastructure project under Cameroon Vision 2035 program and the Growth and Employment Strategy Paper 2010-2029. The $430m project is expected to increase the capacity at two existing hydropower plants on the Sanaga River (Song Loulou and Edea) by130 MW. It will also provide 30 MW for rural electrification of the Eastern Region and unlock access to 6,000 MW of hydraulic potential on the Sanaga River through improved river regulation. It is also expected that when fully operational it will potentially reduce marginal power costs over time to as low as $0.02/kWh (after construction of Nachtigal) compared to $0.09/kWh of alternative gas power. [39]

Democracy, Civil and Individual Liberties

There are a number of indexes that measure democracy and the promotion of civil and individual liberties in countries and territories around the world. Prominent among these are the Democracy Index, the Freedom in the World Index and Global Peace Index.

---

36   https://www.theglobaleconomy.com/rankings/roads_quality/Africa/#Cameroon
37   The GESP set the goal of increasing this energy potentials to 3000 MW by 2020.
38   The World Bank, Harnessing Central Africa's Hydropower Potential, p. 4
39   Idem

The Exercise of Democratic Freedoms

The Democracy Index is compiled by the Economist Intelligence Unit (EIU). The EIU is the research and analysis division of The Economist Group, the sister company of *The Economist* newspaper, created in 1946. The index, published since 2006, is based on 60 indicators grouped in five different categories, measuring pluralism, civil liberties and political culture. In addition to a numeric score (on a scale of 0-10) and a ranking, the index categorizes each country into one of four regime types, namely, full democracies, flawed democracies, hybrid regimes and authoritarian.

Since its inception in 2006 to date, Cameroon's score has averaged 3.39 on 10, which is one point below the Sub-Saharan African average of 4.3 on 10 and more than 2 points below the world average of 5.5 on 10. As a result, Cameroon has consistently been categorized as "authoritarian".

The EIU defines an authoritarian regime as a nation where "...*political pluralism has vanished or is extremely limited*". Such a nation, which could also be described as a dictatorship "*may have some conventional institutions of democracy but with meagre significance, infringements and abuses of civil liberties are commonplace, elections (if they take place) are not fair and free, the media is often state-owned or controlled by groups associated with the ruling regime, the judiciary is not independent, and there are omnipresent censorship and suppression of governmental critics*".[40]

The 2019 Democracy Index ranked Cameroon at 141 out of 167 countries polled, a position it shared with Afghanistan. It is however, important to state that the index also concluded that democracy witnessed a setback globally in 2019.[41]

Freedom House, a US-based Non-Governmental Organization, has been conducting research and advocacy on democracy, political freedom and human rights since its founding in 1941. Its *Freedom in the World* index, published since 1973, assesses the condition of political rights and civil liberties in 195 countries and 15 territories, allowing Freedom House to track global trends in democratic freedoms enshrined in the U.N Declaration of Human Rights.

In 2020, Freedom House adopted a new methodology which measures 10 political rights indicators divided into 3 subcategories, namely, Electoral process, Political Pluralism and participation and Functioning of Government. Fifteen civil liberties indicators divided into 4 subcategories were also added. The subcategories are, Freedom of Expression and Belief, Associational and Organizational Rights, Rule of Law and Personal Autonomy and Individual Rights.

---

40   www.eiu.com
41   "Democracy Index 2019: A Year of Democratic Setbacks and Popular Protest", a report by the Economist Intelligence Unit.

On the basis of the evaluation of these indicators, countries are categorized as 'Free', 'Partly Free' or 'Not Free'.

Since 2015, Cameroon's score in the Freedom in the World Index has averaged 20 on 100, and is categorized as "Not Free". This is far short of the performance of a country like Cote d'Ivoire which is polling above 50 per cent and categorized as "Partly Free", in spite of the fact that it is just emerging from a decade-long armed conflict.[42]

Promotion and Consolidation of Peace

A state's capacity to enhance democratic practices, ensure respect for the rule of law and uphold individual and public liberties can be gauged through its ability and willingness to promote peace and inclusiveness within its borders. This can be achieved in the way the state exercises its authority. Yet, as I mentioned earlier in this chapter, Cameroon's institutions are more extractive than inclusive, to go by Acemoglu and Robinson's standards. When state institutions have been hijacked by a small elite, tailored to the needs and made to serve the interest of a political hegemony, they become unresponsive to the needs and wishes of people. And when people no longer identify with their nation's institutions, those institutions become irrelevant and fragile, leading to the fragility of the state as well.

This is the kind of internal dynamic that is captured in the Global Peace Index and the Fragile States index.

The Global Peace Index (GPI), published by the Institute for Economics & Peace since 2006, measures more than just the presence or absence of war. It captures the absence of violence or the fear of violence across three domains, namely, Safety and Security, Ongoing Conflict, and Militarization. Its safety and security category shows an increased tendency towards authoritarianism worldwide, often characterized by a deterioration in key indicators like *"political terror scale, police rate, and incarceration rate"*.[43] Since 2008, the GPI has categorized the state of peace in Cameroon as "Low". In the 2020 GPI, Cameroon was ranked 38th out 44 Sub Saharan African (SSA) countries, falling within the bottom 10 of countries considered as peaceful in SSA.

The Global Peace Index findings for Cameroon are complemented by those of the Fragile State Index (FSI). The Fragile State Index (formerly the Failed States Index) is published by the Fund for Peace, a US-based Non-Governmental

---

42   www.freedomhouse.org
43   Institute for Economics & Peace. Global Peace Index 2020: Measuring Peace in a Complex World, Sydney, June 2020. Available from: www.visionofhumanity.org

Organization founded in 1957. The Fragile States Index measures the risks and vulnerabilities in 178 countries worldwide. It has become a critical tool for identifying conflict fault-lines and pressures common to nation-states and when those pressures are outweighing the state's capacity to manage them. It is therefore a viable conflict early warning and political assessment tool designed for policymakers and the public in general.[44]

The FSI ranks states from 1-178. The lower the rank the more fragile the state is considered to be and the higher the rank the more sustainable or stable it is deemed to be. In this regard, states are categorized as Sustainable, Stable, Warning and Alert. Cameroon has gone from the 36th position in 2006 to 13th in 2020. Its overall trend during this period is described as "worsening" and the country is categorized as being in the "Alert" stage.

Conclusion

In this chapter I set out to show where we are as a country in some critical areas of our national life: the Economy, Human and Social Development (education, health, poverty, inequality) Governance and Institutional Capacity, Infrastructure (roads and energy), Democracy, Civil and Individual Liberties. As I have been able to demonstrate through analysis of various assessment reports, including those of the government, and globally acclaimed indices, there is hardly any area of the chosen domains of our national life one can point at and say with a modicum of certitude that we have made, or are making, any significant or meaningful progress.

Granted, in the course of the last ten years, there have been palpable attempts to recover from the lost decade of 1985 to 1995, through the drafting and implementation of different flag ship development programs, notably, the Cameroon Vision 2035 and its implementation frameworks like the Growth and Employment Strategy Paper that ended in 2020 and its successor, the National Development Strategy 2030. These programs offer a glimmer of hope that Cameroon may finally be on the path of progress; they are very clear in their vision, in their objectives and in their deliverables. Nonetheless, I still harbor strong doubts as to the government's ability to implement them. My doubts are borne of what I see as policy incongruities and misplaced priorities in their implementation.

I have one symptomatic evidence of this.

---

44   https://fragilestatesindex.org/

Policy Incongruities and Misplaced Priorities

The core objective of Cameroon Vision 2035 is to transform the country into an emerging middle-income economy by 2035. In this regard, the Working Paper of Cameroon Vision 2035 aspirationally states that:

> The status of middle income country will concretize the objective of doubling at least the average income to ensure that Cameroon progresses from a low income to a middle income country by enhancing growth to a two-digit level by 2017 and maintaining this level for a number of years.[45]

The GESP however, lowered the growth expectations of Cameroon Vision 2030 from two-digit growth by 2017 to 5.5 per cent by 2020. These were both very clear, strategic but also achievable targets. But it was in 2017 that the Government, faced with a potentially explosive conflict in its Anglophone regions, preferred a military solution, instead of pursuing political and peaceful options that were available to it in abundance at the time. Development economist, Paul Collier, famously wrote that *"one of the factors known to impede growth is war"*.[46] So it is totally mind-boggling why a government that had set for itself the objective of attaining 5.5 per cent growth by 2020, chose that same time to open up a second war front (after the one against Boko Haram in the Northern regions) even when it was clear that doing so will significantly impede its ability to achieve its growth target. The consequences have been obvious. In 2013 Cameroon's economy was growing at 5.40 per cent but it fell to 4.1 per cent in 2018, according to the government's own assessment, and further contracted to 2.4 per cent in 2020, according to the African Development Bank.

These are the kind of policy incongruities and misplaced priorities that make me doubt if the government shall be able to stay on target with its development programs. It was another development economist, Jeffrey Sachs, who said economic development requires a government oriented towards development.[47] It is common knowledge that the Government of Cameroon has a healthy obsession with politics and "maintenance of law and order"; not with the economy. Very little concern is often directed towards exploring peaceful, cheaper and more

45   Cameroon Vision 2035 Working Paper, February 2009, p. viii

46   Collier, P. (2007). *The Bottom Billion: Why Poor Countries are Failing and what can be done about It.* Oxford: Oxford University Press. p. 17.

47   Sachs, J. (2005). *The End of Poverty: Economic Possibilities of our Times.* New York: Penguin Books p. 59.

sustainable ways of managing conflicts, especially conflicts of the ilk raging in Anglophone Cameroon. Studies have shown that it is cheaper to politically accommodate separatist groups than to fight them militarily.

Beyond the policy incongruities and misplaced priorities are the broader issues of governance and leadership.

The Challenges of Leadership and Governance

Over the course of the last three decades, a good number of strategy papers and development programs, intended to move the country forward, have been churned out. None of them has been successfully implemented for mainly two reasons: first, an archaic governance system ill-adapted to the exigencies of a progressive modern country and second, a leadership that has consistently shown itself as incapable of initiating and managing a change process. Cameroon, it seems, is led by people of an analogue age trying to manage a country in a digital age. So, it is no wonder that it is the leadership that is holding the country back. Someone once told me that in Cameroon, if you have a great idea on how to make things work, do not send it to Unity Palace because if you do, your idea will be killed immediately[48]. Unity Palace, he averred, is the cemetery of great ideas. And so drawing up new development programs and trying to implement them within a governance framework and a leadership paradigm that have long outlived their usefulness is an exercise in futility, akin to the proverbial pouring of new wine into old wine skins.

This is precisely where the renewal of the promise of this nation, and its refounding shall begin: developing a new governing architecture and envisioning a viable leadership model for the country. In the next chapters I shall say how this can be achieved.

---

48   Unity Palace is the seat of the executive branch of government. It is where the President resides and works.

Chapter Three

Untangling the Decentralization Conundrum

Simokoh is a small village of about 5,000 inhabitants, located 10 km east of the Oku subdivisional headquarters of Elak. Its most prominent social infrastructure is its Government Primary School (GPS). In 1998, the government spent tens of millions of francs CFA on a contract to build and equip two new classrooms at the Government Primary School of Simokoh. The objective, of course, was to improve both the learning conditions of the pupils and the working environment of the teachers. The contractor did a marvelous job. Not only did she build and equip the two classrooms in record time, she used the left-over material to renovate and rehabilitate the existing classrooms and toilets that had been built by the parents, even though it was not part of her contract.

By the year 2000, GPS Simokoh was among the best equipped Government Primary Schools in Oku Subdivision in terms of infrastructure. But unfortunately, this important investment made by the government to improve on the learning conditions of the pupils was being wasted because of poor management.

The headmaster of Government Primary School Simokoh in those days was an irresponsible, derelict drunk, who spent most of his time in the drinking parlors in and around Simokoh and the Tadu area. He went about disheveled, unkempt, with a raffia bag perpetually hung across his shoulders in which were sachets of whisky commonly known then as "Nikita". He was hardly ever present in school. And when he showed up, it was to pick up the Parents Teacher Association (PTA) levies and the National Federation of School and College Sports (FENASCO) dues collected from the parents by the teachers. With his pockets lined up, he would promptly go back to his drinking spree.

Since the headmaster was hardly ever there, it follows that the school was poorly managed. The teachers, taking their cue from their boss, were never present in class. For most of the time the learners were left to themselves. The parents became so frustrated that they started withdrawing their children and transferring them to other schools in the vicinity, especially to Government Primary School Mbokeghas, some 3 kilometers away. I need to however, stress that at the time Government Primary School Mbokeghas was nothing but a collection of mud brick structures with dusty floors and rudimentary desks.

I was serving as the Divisional Officer of Oku Subdivision at the time and I could not understand how the government's effort to invest in the education of its young people was being thwarted by the irresponsible actions of a lone individual. I was determined to have that headmaster sacked and replaced by someone with a better and higher sense of duty. It was then that I ran headlong into the complexities of administrative centralization in Cameroon.

In Cameroon, headmasters of elementary schools are appointed and can also only be removed by the National Minister in charge of Basic Education. I remember writing numerous reports to the minister, detailing the unprofessional conduct of the headmaster, describing the sordid and dire situation prevalent at Government Primary School Simokoh and the deleterious effects they were having on the future of the children of that community. I ended my reports with a strong recommendation for the immediate removal and replacement of the head teacher. I never received a response. I was later made aware of the fact that, knowing that I was determined to have him removed, the headmaster had kept some unscrupulous civil servants on the lookout at the Ministry of Basic Education. Each time any of my reports arrived at the Ministry these unscrupulous people (who were obviously on the payroll of the headmaster) made sure the reports were removed and destroyed before they got to the Minister or to any senior managers at the Ministry. By the time I was leaving Oku in September 2000, that Headmaster was still in his post and enrolment at Government Primary School Simokoh had dwindled down considerably.

My failed attempts to have this irresponsible headmaster removed, and thus give value to the government's investment in the education of its young ones, is one of the most frustrating moments in my ten-year tenure as a Field Administrative Officer in Cameroon. At a personal level it opened my eyes to the drawbacks enhanced administrative centralization can have on the lives of ordinary people. I could see palpably, how over-centralization was impeding the satisfactory implementation of the country's socio-economic development programs in a key sector like basic education. I remember asking the question on several occasions: why should mid-level field functionaries like headmasters of elementary schools be appointed at the national level? Why can't the appointment of this category of civil servants be delegated to Regional Governors, who given their proximity to the population, should be able to do so with greater efficiency and efficacy? I was raising these questions because, had that gentleman been appointed by the Regional Governor, I would have physically bundled him into my car, drove him to the Governor's Office in Bamenda, dumped him there and tell the Governor I wasn't going to leave until he relieved that drunk of his duties and appointed a more deserving headmaster for G.P.S Simokoh. That was how frustrated and how infuriated I had become with the entire process of dealing with a corrupt and irresponsible mid-level civil servant who was jeopardizing the future of young Cameroonians and undermining Government education policy and its commitments to the attainment of the Millennium Development Goals.

There are about 12,500 government primary schools scattered all over the national territory, I am told. It is sheer foolhardiness to think that a Minister sitting in the capital can appoint head teachers to all of them and do so effectively and efficaciously.

This story may just be a hint of the nefarious effects of over-centralization in Cameroon. However, it captures in a very practical way its consequences on the wellbeing of communities and its implications for the implementation of government development policies and programs. In the preceding chapters I argued there is hardly any aspect of our national life in which we are making palpable progress: not in education, not in health, not in infrastructure, not in economic growth and poverty alleviation, not in governance, not in the promotion of individual and public liberties. Until and unless we change the way we do business as a state and the way we govern, we are unlikely to attain the objectives set out in our national development programs, especially Cameroon Vision 2035.

This change can only come about through a bold, well planned, re-structuring and re-engineering of Cameroon's governance system. This restructuring and this re-engineering should be such that the responsibility for developing this nation and for guaranteeing its stability is shared equitably among all its citizens at national, regional and local levels. For too long the citizenry of this nation have been mere bystanders and spectators in the decision-making process over issues that touch fundamentally on their everyday lives. Citizen participation, voice and accountable leadership are the pillars of decentralized governance. And it is this decentralized governance model that must inform the process of the re-structuring and the refounding of this nation.

However, for this to happen, we must first of all resolve our decentralization conundrum.

To Decentralize or not to Decentralize

The fall of the Berlin Wall in 1989 followed by the collapse of the Soviet Union in 1991 ushered in a wind of political and economic change around the world. In most African countries, popular movements emerged, demanding an end to one-party autocratic rule; calls for political and economic liberalization and greater democratic freedoms were getting louder. Civil Society activists and the leaders of the nascent political opposition were asking for the reform of the state with fierce urgency. In most of the continent, established political hegemonies and centralized one-party autocracies were being challenged like never before. It was argued that the one-party state had been an unmitigated disaster due largely to corruption, cronyism, and over-centralization and in some instances, its brutality. Even though the one-party state can be said to have assured a veneer of immediate post-independence stability, it however, had failed in its endeavors to promote rapid socio-economic growth and had proven itself inadequate in guaranteeing individual and collective rights and freedoms.

The solution, it was further argued, was a return to multiparty politics (for countries which had had it before) and for a more pluralistic society. This was to be followed by political and economic liberalization and a reform of the governing institutions and structures of the State so as to adapt them to the new socio-political and economic dispensation engendered by the collapse of the Soviet Union, the end of the Cold War and internal popular demands for change.

Among international development agencies and the international finance institutions (like the World Bank and the International Monetary Fund) the emphasis shifted slightly from economic growth to governance as the building blocks of socio-economic development.

Governance and Decentralization

Governance – understood as the institutions and traditions by which and through which authority is exercised in a nation-state – came to sharper focus in the 1990s. Governance as a concept is intricately linked to institutions. So quite predictably, the governance discourse of the 1990s and beyond was framed around state and institutional capacity. In development terms this meant the ability of state institutions to drive growth (measured in terms of a steadily rising GDP) and promote broad-based socio-economic development (understood as continuous improvements in education, health, sanitation, poverty alleviation and measures to curb inequality). It was also about the process by which decisions are made and implemented in a way that responds to the needs of the masses. The responsibility of governments and governing bodies to meet the needs of the masses as opposed to the needs of a select and privileged few is what came to be known broadly as *good governance*.

One-party autocracies, such as existed in most of Sub-Saharan Africa in the 1990s, were characterized by the rule of strongmen as against rule by strong institutions. Under one-party dictatorships the decision making was in the hands of one man or in the hands of a ruling cabal; citizen's voice and participation counted for nothing. By their very nature therefore, they were antithetical to the notions of governance and good government. One way in which better socio-economic development outcomes could be attained and civil and individual liberties guaranteed was to restructure the state such that its institutions became more inclusive and its citizens were actively involved in the decision-making process. This could be attained through enhanced decentralization. Or decentralized governance.

There are many definitions of the concept of decentralization. But the one that best suits the purpose of this treatise is the one given at the Caribbean Conference on Local Government and Decentralization which held in Georgetown Guyana in June 2002. At that conference Keith L Miller defined decentralization as:

> ...the transfer of state/national responsibilities or functions from central government to sub-national levels of government, or from central agencies/offices to regional bodies or branch offices, or to non-governmental organizations or private concerns. It can be described as the redefinition of structures, procedures and practices of governance to be closer to the citizenry.[1]

This definition is very elaborate and all-encompassing as it captures and summarizes both the purpose and the different forms of decentralization, namely, deconcentration, delegation and devolution.

According to Miller, deconcentration, which is sometimes called administrative or bureaucratic decentralization, is the term used when decentralization takes the form of a transfer of functions from the center to regional or branch of an office, but with real decision-making still retained at the center. When the transfer of functions is to a non-governmental or private sector entity (privatization), or

---

1   Miller, K. (2002). *Advantages and Disadvantages of Local Government Decentralization*. Paper presented at the Caribbean Conference on Local Government and Decentralization, Georgetown, Guyana.

to a government agency over which government exercises limited control, this is referred to as delegation. And lastly, devolution occurs where the transfer of any function or responsibility involves both administrative as well as political/decision-making authority. This is usually to a sub-national level of government, which can then be said to enjoy autonomy in respect to the devolved subjects/functions, provided that nothing else inhibits the exercise of such autonomy (e.g., excessive financial dependency or lack of local administrative/technical capacity).

Conflicting Notions of Decentralization in Cameroon

In Cameroon, decentralization has always been a thorny issue since independence. Given their different historical experiences derived from their different colonial legacies, decentralization has been understood, experimented and practiced in different ways in the Francophone and Anglophone parts of the country.

As I noted in Chapter One, Francophone Cameroon at independence on 1 January 1960 inherited from the French, a highly centralized Jacobin state model where power was concentrated at the center, and in the hands of an executive president. This state model fitted squarely into the designs and intentions of Ahmadou Ahidjo, its first President, a man prone to visceral autocratic tendencies and imbued with a near intestinal aversion for sharing power.

As a colonial power, France opted for what it called a "prudent' and a "diversified" decentralization for French Cameroun.[2] Accordingly, between 1960 and 1967 Ahidjo passed a series of laws and executive orders regulating and defining the role of local authorities in East (Francophone) Cameroon. As Alain Valette points out, this multiplicity of texts, promulgated and implemented within very short intervals of each other, soon lent themselves to confusion and contradiction. In East Cameroon, councils were divided into three categories, *Commune de Plein Exercice* (or City Councils), *Commune de moyen exercice* (or urban councils) and *Commune Rural Mixte* (or mixed rural councils). Whatever the category, the councils were meant to function under strict central government control and supervision. Even though councilors were generally elected, mayors were appointed by presidential decree or by an order of the Secretary of State for Interior depending on the category of the council. Interestingly, there was no requirement to choose the mayor from among the elected councilors. This gave rise to the phenomenon of *Sous Prefet-Maire* where District Heads and Divisional Officers were appointed to serve as Mayors of Rural Councils.

2   See Alain Valette: "L'organisation Communale au Cameroun Oriental", *Bulletin Officiel des Communes, 1967*

A certain duality of functions was also put in place in the City Councils where there was an elected chairperson functioning side-by-side with a Government Delegate appointed by the Central Government. The Government Delegate exercised full executive authority over the council while the elected Chairperson was reduced to a figure head whose sole role was to preside over council meetings convened at the behest of the Government Delegate. The Secretary of State for the Interior and the Field Administrative Officers (Prefects) exercised strict day-to-day control and supervision over the councils. A council, elected by universal suffrage, could be summarily dissolved by a decree of the President or by an order of the Secretary of State for Interior. Moreover, Councils could not even collect the taxes ceded to them by the central government. Council taxes were collected by the local administrative officers and local offices of the Inland Revenue Service and then remitted to the Councils. It is therefore evident that in Francophone Cameroon, councils as decentralized governance units, were never meant to exercise any meaningful authority. Given Ahidjo's penchant and preference for a strong centralized government, the emasculation of councils and the lack of political will to pursue decentralization as a governance system was fairly predictable.

In Anglophone Cameroon, decentralization was understood and practiced differently. This difference was due to clear distinctions between the French and British colonial systems. Veronique Dimier, a leading expert on French and British colonial administration policies, eloquently sums up these differences in these words:

> The French colonial system is usually depicted by historians as a very centralised, unified and bureaucratic system whose aim was the assimilation of native people and whose method was direct rule, namely the destruction of native authorities and their replacement by French officers. The main task of these officers was to act as the typical civil servants of a bureaucratic state: they would mainly enforce the law prescribed by Paris regardless of native society's customs. If they happened to use the local chiefs they would merely nominate them according to their loyalty and would turn them into French civil servants.

The British did it differently. Through its policy of Indirect Rule, which was itself conceptually derived from the principles of Sacred Trust enshrined in the

Covenant of the League of Nations and Lord Lugard's Dual Mandate,[3] the British Colonial Administration instituted a system that, according to Dimier, was regarded as:

> ...very decentralised, pragmatic and based on indirect rule. Through its native policy it sought to respect native customs as long as they were not opposed to British conceptions of civilisation. It also tried to respect the real native chiefs chosen by their people, and rule through them by means of persuasion, advice and education.[4]

Dimier cites Cameroon as a good example of the difference between French and British models of decentralization implemented during the colonial period.

However, renowned academic, Prof Mahmood Mamdani in his acclaimed work, *Citizen and Subject* sees both Direct and Indirect rule more as alternative but complementary ways of controlling the natives during the colonial period. In that regard, he writes:

> Direct rule was the form of urban civil power. It was about the exclusion of natives from civil freedoms guaranteed to citizens in civil society. Indirect rule however, signified a rural tribal authority. It was about incorporating natives into a state enforced customary order.[5]

Mamdani holds that when reformulated, both direct and indirect rule were nothing but variants of despotism, "the former centralized, the latter decentralized". This is what Mamdani calls "decentralized despotism", which, according to him, is one of the root causes of the failure of statehood in post-colonial Africa.[6]

The Good Government Mandate

Chapter 22 of the Covenant of the League of Nations laid down very broadly basic principles of "good government" that Mandate Powers were supposed to

3   Lugard, L. (1922). *The Dual Mandate in British Tropical Africa*. London: Frank Case and Co Ltd. pp. 60-62.

4   See Dimier, V. (2004). On Good Colonial Government: Lessons from the League of Nations. *Global Society, 18*(3), 279-299.

5   Mamdani, M. (2004). *Citizen and Subject: Contemporary Africa and the Legacy of Late Colonialism*. Kampala: Fountain Publishers. p.18

6   Ibid

observe in the mandated territories. With regard to colonies and territories that had lost their colonial tutelage as a consequence of the First World War and that were not in a position to govern themselves as sovereign states, chapter 22 asserted that "...*there should be applied the principle that the well-being and development of such peoples form a sacred trust of civilization...*". This is what came to be known as the "good government" principle or "democratic imperialism".

Lord Lugard, a former British Governor of Nigeria (1914-1919) and British representative to the Permanent Mandate Commission set up under Chapter 22 of the Covenant of the League of Nations (1922 -1936) often touted Britain's policy of indirect rule as being more reflective of the good government principle of the mandate, namely, government for the welfare of native peoples. On the other hand, Lord Lugard described France as exploiting her colonies and deriving her colonial policy from principles which were clearly condemned by the League of Nations, and that is, the idea of colonies as mere properties serving the interests of the colonial power.

Native Administration as Decentralized Governance in Anglophone Cameroon

The British started implementing Indirect Rule (also called Native Administration) in the League of Nations Mandated Territory of Southern Cameroons in the late 1920s. This was done principally through the setting up of Native Authorities. The Native Authorities were organized around already existing, strong traditional chieftaincy institutions known in the Grassfields region as Fondoms (headed by Fons) and in the Coastal region as Chiefdoms (headed by chiefs). The Fons and Chiefs were appointed as the Heads of the "Native Authorities" and charged with exercising governing responsibility over their people according to their customs and traditions. They were in charge of collecting poll taxes and ensuring the delivery of basic services at the grassroots. Examples of such services included education, justice, health and sanitation and land development. The Native Authorities created and managed elementary schools, and health centers (or "dispensaries" as they were known at the time), courts and markets. They also undertook community projects like the building of inter-village roads. Native Authorities were the precursors of municipal governments as we know them today. More importantly, and as Prof Anthony Ndi has pointed out, Native Authorities instilled within the people of Anglophone Cameroon the "*spirit of self-reliance, self-actualization and self-rule*" that will become a permanent and defining feature of their way of life.[7]

---

7   Ndi, A. (2016). *The Golden Age of Southern Cameroons: Vital Lessons for Cameroon*. Denver:

The contrasts between French and British colonial policies and governing systems defined the different ways Francophone Cameroon and Anglophone Cameroon understood and approached the question of decentralization after Unification in October 1961. These differences have led to a decentralization conundrum that has remained unresolved to this day. But the fact of the matter remains that it is the French Cameroon model of decentralization that has always prevailed.

Decentralization within the Unitary State Structure and Beyond

In 1974, two years after the abolition of the Federation, Law No. 74-23 bearing on the Organization of Councils was enacted. The law was basically a recycled version of different laws passed in East Cameroon between 1960 and 1967 organizing local councils in that federated state: The categorization of councils, the mode of designation of mayors, central government control and supervision of councils, the limited responsibility of councils, central government control over council finances etc., - which were prominent features of local governance system in East Cameroon – were all replicated almost word for word into the 1974 law. Very little effort was made to accommodate the decentralized governance principles and models that existed in West (Anglophone) Cameroon. In fact, it was explicitly stated that Law No. 74-23 had abrogated the Local Authorities Ordinance, CAP 140 of 1948, which was the main legislative framework for decentralized governance in all British colonies, dominations and protectorates, including Southern/West Cameroon.

Constitutional Reform and Decentralization in the 1990s

The 1990s in Cameroon was marked by demands both from within and without for political pluralism, economic liberalization, greater democratic freedoms and, in a general manner, the reform of the state. In addition, the Anglophone minority which had complained of marginalization for decades, became very forceful in its demands for greater autonomy and better protection of its minority status, in a manner consistent with the promises and resolutions of the Foumban Conference of 1961. Initially President Biya ignored calls for reform, arguing that the institutions of the state were functioning normally and so needed no reform. But when the opposition bloc instituted ghost towns to pressure him to convene a sovereign national conference to discuss the future of the country, he caved in somewhat, and convened a Tripartite Conference

Spears Media Press. p.33.

between the Opposition, the Civil Society and the Government. The Tripartite Conference held in Yaoundé from 30 October to 9 November 1991. It came up with broad proposals for a process for electoral and constitutional reform. The question of decentralization for the country and a self-governing status of the former federated state of West Cameroon was again a focus of discussions.

The 1996 Constitution, an upshot of the Tripartite Conference, asserted that Cameroon shall be governed on the basis of a "decentralized unitary state". In this regard, article 55 provided for the creation of regional and local authorities to be freely administered by elected councils. These authorities enjoyed the status of corporate bodies under public law and were granted administrative and financial autonomy in the management of regional and local affairs. The mandate of the regional and local authorities was principally to promote the economic, social, health, educational, cultural and sports development of the said authorities.

As plausible as these changes might have seem, their slow implementation soon exposed the government's lack of political will to truly pursue decentralization. This lack of political will was evident in the lack of urgency in instituting the requisite legal and regulatory framework needed for the regional and local authorities to effectively take off. For instance, the Constitution was adopted in 1996, yet it was not until 2004, eight years later, that government saw the need to pass Law No. 2004/017 of 22 July 2004 on the orientation of decentralization; Law No 2004 / 018 of 22 July 2004 to lay down rules applicable to Councils; and Law No 2004/019 of 22 July 2004 to lay down rules applicable to regions. It took another five years (2009) to issue Decree No 2009/248 of 05 August 2009 to lay down Conditions for the Partial Financing of Decentralization. It was not until 2011 – fifteen years since the Constitution was adopted and seven years after the decentralization laws were passed – that a series of Prime Ministerial Orders were issued fixing modalities for the implementation of certain competences transferred from the national government to local authorities. In all it took about sixteen years for the government to develop the baseline legal and regulatory framework for decentralization.

Inadequacy of the 1996 Decentralization Framework

As if government's feet-dragging on the decentralization question was not enough, when the orientation law was made public in 2004, it fell far short of the expectations of Cameroonians. There was nothing revolutionary about it. Quite telling was the level of central government (or State) control of regional and local authorities, which many consider as a violation of the constitutional principle of the "free administration" of these authorities. Prof Ndiva Kofele-Kale summed it up beautifully when he noted that:

> ...the form of decentralisation favoured by Cameroon's legislator operates in such a way that the powers purportedly devolved to regional and local governments are severely circumscribed by an intrusive and ubiquitous central government.[8]

Palpable proof that the government was not prepared to cede responsibility to Local Authorities can be seen in the execution of the public investment budget. As I said in Chapter Two, in 2010 - fourteen years after the Constitution was adopted and six years after the decentralization laws were passed – the Central Government was still responsible for the execution of more than 90 per cent of the public investment budget to the detriment of local councils. I am not sure the situation is any different today. In fact the most tangible "progress" made in the pursuit of decentralization in twenty-four years (1996 to 2020) was to rename the provinces as "regions" and to re-appoint its Governors. Even though the Regional Authorities were finally operationalized in 2020, under a new law, they are still subjected to the same "intrusive and ubiquitous" central government control that Prof Ndiva Kofele-Kale alluded to in the quote above. I shall come back to this in greater detail, later in this chapter.

Decentralized Governance and the Management of Community Grievances

In 2016, the populations of the North-West and South-West (Anglophone) Regions took to the streets to protest against marginalization, especially in the education and judicial sectors. The protests were led by teachers' and lawyers' associations. Initially, the teachers and lawyers demanded a return to the pre-1972 two-state federation, as the only way to end the marginalization of Anglophones. A return to the federal system, it was argued, would offer better guarantees for the protection of Anglophone minority rights and the preservation of the Anglo-Saxon way of life derived from its unique colonial heritage. When attempts at dialogue failed, the government, as is usually the case, reacted with a brutal crackdown. By mid-2017, the conflict had evolved into a bloody armed struggle. The demand for federation soon morphed into a demand for secession.

8   See Kofele-Kale, N. (2011). Local governance under Cameroon's decentralisation regime: is it all sound and fury signifying nothing? *Commonwealth Law Bulletin*, *37*(3), 513-530.

The Grand National Dialogue and the Anglophone Problem

Unable to contain the violence in Anglophone Cameroon and faced with pressure from within and from without to seek a political pathway for ending the armed conflict, the government convened a Grand National Dialogue, to address the grievances of the Anglophones. The dialogue held from 30 September to 4 October 2019 and one of its main recommendations was for the government to implement an enhanced decentralization program for the country with a "Special Status" for the North-West and South-West Regions.

And so, just like it happened at the Tripartite Conference nearly three decades earlier, decentralization was again recommended as a viable option of how to move the country forward. It was also hoped that the "Special Status" shall accommodate the grievances of the Anglophone minority and mollify its extremist fringe calling for secession. In December 2019, a little over two months after the end of the dialogue, Law No 2019/024 was passed instituting the General Code of Regional and Local Authorities. Regional Council elections were held in December 2020, followed by the "installation" of its chairpersons soon after. This marked the effective operationalization of the Regional Authorities, twenty-four years after they were first enshrined in the Constitution.

Perhaps it is still premature to say, but compared to the 2004 Law on Decentralization, the government seemed to be keen to expedite the implementation of the General Code of Regional and Local Authorities. But for real progress to be made, the government shall have to, first, overcome its own recurrent fear that devolution might elicit an appetite for secession and, second, it will have to deal with the innate impulses of its own elite to hold onto central authority. I harbor strong doubts that the government shall be able to overcome these two hurdles and pursue its devolution agenda. While the government is prevaricating over decentralization the population continues to suffocate under the weight of an archaic over-centralized Jacobin state model that has clearly gotten out of control.

None of the decentralization frameworks experimented since the advent of the unitary state in 1972 to date have proven adequate in addressing the problems that President Ahidjo advanced as reasons for abolishing the federation. Not even the General Code of Regional and Local Authorities. Apart from the creation of a "Public Independent Conciliator" and the reinstitution of the House of Chiefs in the Anglophone Regions, the Code offers very little novelty from the point of view of doctrine and policy orientation. Conceptually, it is nothing but a mere reorganization of the central government and a rehash of past decentralization frameworks that were in force in the country since reunification in 1961. So it may not work and the decentralization conundrum shall persist. I shall elaborate on why, later in this chapter.

Proposed Decentralization Framework

What this country needs is a well thought-out decentralization framework based on its history and attuned to the exigencies of building a united, modern, progressive, inclusive, democratic state; a framework that can restore and renew the dream and the promises on which this nation was founded and built. In other words, a decentralization framework that shall form the basis for the refoundation of this nation. The kind of decentralization agenda I am proposing shall aim at achieving the following outcomes:

* Enhanced state capacity for the promotion of socio-economic development
* Adequately addressing both the Anglophone Problem and the Southern Cameroons Question.
* Sustainably addressing community grievances and perceived developmental imbalances.
* Improved grassroots democratic governance through a redistribution of power – greater ownership and voice, accountability, inclusiveness, empowerment and civic participation in decision-making and implementation.
* Renewed political agency through asserting the primacy of citizen rights over state prerogative.
* Improved delivery of basic social services especially at the local level.

To achieve these outcomes, I propose the following as core components of the decentralization framework that should constitute the basis for the refoundation of the Cameroon nation.

Elected Regional Governments

After six decades of experimenting with appointed bureaucrats and sometimes overzealous, colonial-style administrators clad in military-style uniforms "commanding" their fellow citizens, I believe the Cameroonian people are now mature enough to freely govern themselves through a full-fledged autonomous or semi-autonomous regional government of their own choosing. The Regional Government shall comprise a Governor and a legislative assembly both elected by direct universal suffrage. Governors elected by direct universal suffrage and exercising full executive authority over their regions will obviously have greater legitimacy and shall be accountable to a local electorate, not solely to the President of the Republic. The present "Regional Delegations" should be transformed into full-fledged Regional Ministries headed by Regional Ministers appointed by the Governor. Together with the Governor, the Regional Ministers shall constitute the Regional Executive Council, which shall be the executive arm of the Regional Government.

I know the idea of elected Regional Governors exercising full executive authority over their regions and primarily accountable to the people may sound outlandish, strange and near impossible to some Cameroonians, especially those of the Francophone Regions. But it won't be to be to those of the Anglophone Regions. Since 1954, Southern Cameroons (as a self-governing territory) and later West Cameroon (as a federated state) had already successfully experimented with a decentralized governance system, where its Chief Executive – The Premier/ Prime Minister – and members of his government were all elected members of the House of Assembly. The fact that the members of government were first and foremost elected members of the House of Assembly meant that they knew intuitively that they were accountable, first, to the people (who elected them) and, second, to the Prime Minister (who appointed them). Ideally, this dual level of accountability strengthens legitimacy and enhances the performance of public office holders. Most importantly, it stands in sharp contrast to the current practice where public officials, including government ministers, only act *"sur les tres hautes instructions de la plus haute hierarchie"*.

A Regional House of Assembly, elected by direct universal suffrage and exercising a wide range of legislative functions devolved to it by the Constitution, shall constitute the legislative arm of the Regional Government.

Both the Constitution and the General Code of Regional and Local Authorities uphold the principle of the free administration of regional and local authorities by "elected organs". A full-fledged regional government is a better reflection of this principle.

Since the early nineties, the Cameroon Government has been grappling with how best to deal with demands from its Anglophone minority for a return to the 1961 federation, and of recent, growing attempts at outright secession. In April 1993, Anglophone Cameroonians from all walks of life convened in Buea in what was billed as an All Anglophone Conference (AAC). The conference was convened for the purpose of developing a common Anglophone position to be presented at a National Debate on Constitutional Reform that had been summoned, pursuant to the resolutions of the Tripartite Conference of 1991. This position was clearly and unequivocally stated in the final declaration of the All Anglophone Conference. In that declaration, known as The Buea Declaration, conference participants noted that the imposition of the unitary state on Anglophone Cameroonians in 1972 was *"unconstitutional, illegal and a breach of faith"* and the only acceptable redress to that wrong was *"a return to the original form of government of the reunified Cameroon"*. To that end it enjoined all Anglophone Cameroonians to work for *"the restoration of a federal constitution and a federal form of government which takes cognizance of the bicultural nature of Cameroon ..."*[9]

The All Anglophone Conference followed up this declaration with the drafting of a federal constitution which it hoped to present to the Constitutional Drafting Committee. The Chairperson of the drafting Committee refused to have the draft tabled for discussion and the Anglophone members of the Committee mandated by the AAC had to walk out. As a result of the arrogance and intransigence of the Francophone head of the drafting committee, when Anglophones met in Bamenda in 1994 for the Second All Anglophone Conference, some were already calling for a "zero option", namely, outright secession.

It was quite clearly in an attempt to stem these growing calls for a federation and secession coming from Anglophone Cameroon that the government settled for a "decentralized unitary state" system in the 1996 Constitution. But as I have said earlier in this chapter, there was never any strong political will from the government to meaningfully decentralize, considering the time it took to set up the legal framework for implementing decentralization. It was nothing but a political gimmick aimed at buying time. I am sure the government was convinced that with time these calls for a federation or for secession will dissipate and then miraculously disappear. Well, they didn't, because in 2016 the calls came back via protests, this time led by the teachers and lawyers; the demands were the same as in 1993: a return to the federal system. By 2017 the protests had turned violent, with armed factions fighting for outright "independence". Unable to contain the violence, the government sought a political approach. In 2019, following a Grand National Dialogue convened to seek a peaceful outcome to the violent conflict in Anglophone Cameroon, it passed the General Code of Regional and Local Authorities. The Code abrogated the 2004 Decentralizations Laws, which were meant to operationalize the decentralized unitary state structure, but which had largely remained unimplemented for fifteen years. Without a modicum of doubt, the Code, like the Decentralization Law before it, was intended as some sort of a "peace offering" to Anglophone Cameroonians.

This explains why the Code established a "special status" for the North-West

---

9   The Buea Declaration of the All Anglophone Conference, issued by the Conference Rapporteurs, Ekontang Elad and Francis Wache.

and South-West regions *"based on their language specificity and historical heritage"*.[10] But it is important to stress that in matters of decentralization, the historical heritage of Anglophone Cameroon is that of a self-governing territory, which had a flourishing Westminster-style democracy, anchored on a functional decentralized governance system, derived from the British colonial policy of Indirect Rule. The so-called "special status" doesn't come anywhere close to restoring that heritage. Here is why.

First, the Code gives to the Regional Governors, in their capacity as "Representative of the State" wide ranging powers of control and supervision over the regional authorities. The President of the Regional Council, an elected official, is placed in a subordinate position to the Governor, an appointed bureaucrat. The preponderance of the authority of the Governors over the Chairpersons of Regional Councils was made clear, when soon after their election, the Regional Chairpersons were "installed" by the Governors. This is not the "historical heritage" of Anglophone Cameroon. Rather, it is a replication of the same nefarious state of affairs that existed in Buea (the seat of government of West Cameroon) in the 1960s where, soon after unification in 1961, Ahmadou Ahidjo appointed a Francophone "Federal Inspector of Administration" to "oversee" the elected Prime Minister of West Cameroon and his government. It is important to remember that the Prime Minister and his entire cabinet were all elected members of the House of Assembly. Anglophone Cameroonians in their entirety resented that arrangement that was clearly at odds with their understanding of the principles and practice of decentralized governance, and which sought to undermine their elected leaders. It was as if a Francophone Cameroun Administrator had replaced the British Colonial Administrators in West Cameroon.

Second, when I first read the General Code of Regional and Local Authorities, I was immediately struck by the provisions of Section 2 (2) which stipulate that Regional and Local Authorities *"shall carry out their activities with due respect for national unity and solidarity, territorial integrity and the primacy of the State"*. It is the words "the primacy of the state" that caught my attention. The principle of the "primacy of the state" is a French Public Law concept that places state prerogatives above citizens' rights. Within the context of decentralization, what the principle of the primacy of the state does is that it puts in place a Principal-Agent paradigm in which the State is the Principal and the Regional and Local Authorities are its agents, executing its will. This is just another form

---

10 Section 3 (1) of the General Code for Regional and Local Authorities

of deconcentration, not devolution, as claimed in Section 5: (1) of the Code.[11] Devolution implies the relinquishing of political power. As Keith Miller held at the 2002 Caribbean Conference on Local Government and Decentralization in Guyana, when local governance institutions *"operate essentially as agents of central government rather than as instruments of local self-expression, this in reality constitutes deconcentration rather than devolution"*. [12] In their present set-up it is hard to see how regional and local authorities that function as agents of the central government and are subjected to the strict controls of the agents of the central government can be true mechanisms for local self-expression, voice and accountability.

The principle of the primacy of the state and the Principal-Agent model it begets has far reaching implications for the rules of political agency and for the supposed Special Status accorded to the North West and South-West Regions by the General Code. Section 3 (3) of the General Code stipulates that *"the special status shall also entail respect for the peculiarity..."* and *"...consideration of the specificities of the Anglo Saxon legal system based on common law"*.

Since the 13th century, the Anglo-Saxon legal system has developed frameworks and instruments to safeguard individual freedom against the use of arbitrary state authority. Since the State is often defined in terms of its ability to use violence, it follows that the exercise of state power inherently lends itself to abuse and arbitrariness vis-à-vis its citizens. That is why whenever the rights of a citizen is in conflict with the prerogatives of the State, common law judges have always acted to uphold the rights of the citizen. They do this based on time-tested instruments and principles like the Magna Carta, the Writ of Habeas Corpus, the Bill of Rights, the presumption of innocence, equality of all before the law etc. These are the foundational instruments and core principles of the rule of law and the basis of Common Law as we know them today. So when the General Code espouses the "primacy of the state" as against "the primacy of the people", and then extends this notion to the North-West and South West Regions, it essentially contradicts the claim that the special status takes into account the specificities of the Anglo-Saxon legal system based on common law. For the special status provision to be seen as aggregating Anglo-Saxon culture

---

11   Section of 5(1) of the General Code on Regional and Local Authorities stipulates that "Decentralization shall consist of devolution by the State of special power and appropriate resources to local authorities"

12   See Miller, K. (2002). *Advantages and Disadvantages of Local Government Decentralization.* Paper presented at the Caribbean Conference on Local Government and Decentralization, Georgetown, Guyana.

and traditions it needs to reverse the Principal-Agent hierarchical paradigm such that THE PEOPLE are the Principal and the Regional and Local Authorities are their Agents.

This is very important because at the heart of the Anglophone Problem – which the special status purports to address - is the issue of self-determination (understood as the process by which a group of people, usually possessing a certain degree of national consciousness, form their own state and choose their own government). There is the pervasive feeling among Anglophone Cameroonians that their self-determination process was derailed when the Federation was abolished in 1972, and has since remained incomplete. I believe that only a properly elected Regional Government, answerable to the people that elected it and deriving its authority from a Schedule of the Constitution, can come close to restoring the historical legacy of the North-West and South West Regions in matters of decentralization. An elected Regional Government shall re-ignite in Anglophone Cameroonians the assurance that their self-determination process is once more on track.

Not only Anglophone Cameroonians have been complaining of neglect and marginalization from the Central Government. Other regions may be less vocal and less militant in articulating their grievances. But they do speak, albeit, with timidity. In the past the populations of the Greater North region and the East Region (all regions with some of the worse human development indicators in the country) have on several occasions petitioned the Central Government to complain about neglect and marginalization. And on each occasion the elite from those regions, especially those affiliated to the ruling Cameroon People's Democratic Movement (CPDM) party, have always dismissed the petitioners as inconsequential rabble-rousers with no mandate to speak for the people. Nonetheless the feeling of neglect remains palpable. A sincere decentralization program, with a regional government and a regional legislative assembly elected by direct universal suffrage should be able to address some of these grievances before they boil over and mutate into armed conflict, as is the case now in Anglophone Cameroon.

Enhanced Capacity for the Enforcement of Municipal Laws

The Bamenda Main Market is located on the busiest street, Commercial Avenue in the City of Bamenda. The market brings together thousands of people every day - buyers, sellers, commuters, taxi-drivers, motorbike taxis etc. The place is always a beehive of activity at any time of the day. At 5 pm, when the market closes, the hustling and bustling reach a frenzy. But curiously it is also at 5 pm that the national police officers who are always on duty at the market, also clock out. In other words, the police sign off for the day just at the time when their presence is most needed. The reason for this is simple. Even though the police officers on duty at the market are performing duties of a municipal character, they are attached to the Central Police Precinct. And even though that Precinct's jurisdiction covers most of the City of Bamenda, it does not report to the Mayor. This in effect means that police officers carrying out municipal police duties do so with little coordination with, and sometimes with no input from, City managers. This lack of coordination between the police and city managers is not unique to Bamenda. And it is one reason why municipal laws and regulations are so hard to enforce, making the country's towns and cities look like lawless jungles.

The first thing that strikes any first-time visitor to a Cameroonian city or town is the unprecedented levels of disorder and lawlessness. This can be readily seen in the non-respect of building codes and zoning laws and the Highway Code; the anarchical occupation of public spaces including streets and sidewalks, non-respect of basic parking regulations, non-removal of garbage from the streets and over-crowding. Most of this is due to the inability of Mayors to enforce their own laws and regulations. Section 216 of the General Code of Regional and Local Authorities authorizes Mayors to create a "Council Police" which shall be charged with ensuring public order, safety, tranquility, security and cleanliness. The Council Police as it currently exists in most municipalities is largely a makeshift administrative outfit without any judicial enforcement authority. They are recruited by the Councils, with little or no basic training; they are not issued any weapons (including non-lethal weapons) and they have no powers of arrest. It is hard to imagine how "police" can effectively ensure security and public order without those basic tools. The level of lawlessness and disorder in Cameroon's towns and cities are such that it shall require a different but more robust approach to policing and enforcement of municipal laws and regulations, if Mayors are to keep the country's cities and towns safe, clean and orderly.

I propose a two-track approach for strengthening the capacity of Mayors and municipal executives to effectively enforce municipal laws and regulations in such a way as to ensure public order, safety, tranquility, security and cleanliness.

First, I recommend the detachment of National Police units to cities and municipalities. These units shall assume the appellation of "Municipal Police Service" and shall be commanded by an officer at the rank of Superintendent of Police or Senior Superintendent of Police depending on the size of the detachment. The Commander shall have a hard reporting line to the mayor and a soft reporting line to the Regional Delegate of National Security. The current "council police" could then be retrofitted to serve as auxiliaries of the Municipal Police Service. The setting up of the Municipal Police Service shall be a joint venture between the municipalities and the Central Government. The Central Government shall train, equip and pay the municipal police service, while the cities and municipalities shall provide appropriate facilities, vehicles and pay bonuses and other allowances to the officers as stipulated by law. The municipal police service shall be wholly dedicated to enforcing city and municipal laws and regulations under the direction of the mayor and municipal executives. In that regard, it shall have powers to arrest and detain law breakers, in the same way as the National Police. Municipal Police units can be experimented in cities and municipalities of at least 400,000 inhabitants at a ratio of one officer for every 1000 citizens for a start.

Second, to complement and complete the work of the Municipal Police Service, I recommend the setting up of Municipal Courts. These courts, to be headed by first or second scale magistrates, shall be wholly dedicated to the judicial enforcement of municipal laws and regulations in timely and expeditious manner, especially those characterized as simple offences in the Penal Code. Chapter 369(10) of the Penal Code punishes any infringement of or failure to conform to *"any legally made and correctly published regulation or order of the municipal authority"*. This is essentially a 3rd class misdemeanor but which can be re-classified as fourth class. When so re-classified, the defaulter shall be liable to a fine of from 4,000 FCFA to 25,000 FCFA or imprisonment for from five to ten days or both such imprisonment and fine. Quite clearly, the fines and imprisonment terms are too small to create any real deterrence. They shall have to be reviewed and adapted to the onerous challenge of bringing back order and curbing lawlessness in the nation's towns and cities. I believe that the judicial enforcement of such provisions of the Penal Code by Municipal Courts shall create a deterrence that could be critical in curbing the rot in the nation's urban centers. As with the Municipal Police Service, I also propose that the setting up of these municipal courts should be a partnership between the central government and the cities and municipalities desiring them. The central government shall recruit, train, deploy and pay the magistrates and the registry staff, while the cities and municipalities shall be responsible for providing offices and courtrooms, vehicles, bonuses, allowances and running cost of the courts.

Setting up proper Municipal Police Services and Municipal Courts can be done without an enormous extra financial burden on the part of the Central Government and the Local Authorities. It may require only the mobilization, retooling, repurposing and redeployment of existing human resources from within the Police and Judiciary corps. Any supplementary costs could be covered by the Decentralization Fund.

Improved State Capacity

There is this nagging fear within the Cameroonian governing class that decentralization shall dilute and diminish the power, the influence and the capacity of the State. True to its strong adherence to the jacobinist approach to statehood, since independence, the ruling elite has always understood a strong state to mean a heavily centralized state in which power is concentrated in the executive. As I have had occasion to point out earlier in this chapter, it is this understanding of the nature of statehood that has led the country down the path of authoritarianism and dictatorship. This is the kind of mindset that adds further to the nation's decentralization conundrum. For decentralization to be a viable entry point for the refoundation of the Cameroon nation, it must serve to improve and strengthen state capacity from the bottom up.

Scholars and governance experts may not agree on a universally acceptable definition of "state capacity" but they have a common understanding of its constituent elements. These elements are derived in part from the Weberian definition of the state as an organization imbued with the monopoly of the legitimate use of force over a given territory. This definition is of course wedded to the notion that the core function of the state is to maintain order and to prevent widespread, large-scale violence, especially civil wars and secession.

In its most basic sense *state capacity* - also referred to as "state strength" – refers to the aptitude of the state to formulate and implement policies that guarantee the security and the social and economic wellbeing of its citizens. Some scholars prefer the term "state efficacy" understood as:

> .. the efficiency of the bureaucracy and public servants, roles and respon-
> sibilities of local and regional governments, including the administrative
> and technical skills of government, effectiveness of policy and program
> formulation, governing capacity, and effective use of resources.[13]

Standing in parallel to the concept of state capacity or state strength is of

---

13   Faguet, J.-P., Fox, A. M., & Poeschl, C. (2014). *Does decentralization strengthen or weaken the state? Authority and social learning in a supple state.* London School of Economics and Political Science, London, UK: Department of International Development.

course the concept of "state weakness". The Brookings Institution defines weak states as:

> … countries that lack the essential capacity and/or will to fulfill four sets of critical government responsibilities: fostering an environment conducive to sustainable and equitable economic growth; establishing and maintaining legitimate, transparent, and accountable political institutions; securing their populations from violent conflict and controlling their territory; and meeting the basic human needs of their population.[14]

Based on this definition, the Brookings Institution in 2008 published its Index of State Weakness in the Developing World which ranked all 141 developing countries according to their relative performance in four critical spheres: economic, political, security, and social welfare. Cameroon was ranked at number 29, immediately below Nigeria and immediately above Yemen, and classified as "weak" and with a very poor showing in the politics sphere.

On their part, researchers at Russia's National Research University Higher School of Economics have developed an index for measuring state capacity based on three core dimensions: coercive (ensuring external security and internal order); extractive (financial resources, including taxation, available to the state); administrative-bureaucratic (quality of administrative and bureaucratic institutions). These three core dimensions are further measured against six indicators as follows: Military expenditures for ensuring external security (as a % of GDP); aggregated indicator of violence control inside the country (statistics of domestic murders and victims of domestic conflicts expressed in terms of number of cases per 100,000 of population); collectability of revenue taxes as a percentage of GDP; aggregate income of the state budget as a percentage of GDP; World Governance Indicators including Government Electiveness, Regulatory Quality, Rule of Law, and Control of Corruption; Share of shadow economy as a percentage of GDP. Based on the information gathered, the researchers were able to create a State Capacity Index and compile an international ranking of 142 countries. The ranking refers to the best performing states as "leaders" and refers to the least performing ones as "outsiders'. In outsider countries all state capacity indicators are weak or close to minimal, but with a maintained violence control function. Cameroon is ranked in this category.

---

14   Rice, S. E., & Patrick, S. (2008). *Index of State Weakness in the Developing World.* Retrieved from The Brookings Institution, Washington, DC

In addition to these indices, and as I pointed out in chapter two, various internal government reports and analyses from international development and funding agencies like the World Bank and the IMF have routinely cast doubts on the Cameroon government's capacity to achieve economic growth and promote broad-based social development. The country did not meet its commitments under the Millennium Development Goals. And if it continues along the same trajectory, it is most likely not to attain the Sustainable Development Goals and the aspirations set out in its own flagship development agenda: Cameroon Vision 2035. The reason why the country is not meeting its socio-economic goals is simple: a heavy, top-down, inert, corrupt and incompetent bureaucracy that has shown itself as incapable of delivering basic services to the population in a timely and cost-effective manner. The State (usually understood within the Cameroonian context to mean the Central Government) has taken on too many responsibilities than it can manage. And yet it continues to be reticent about meaningfully sharing these responsibilities with its other components.

To reverse this trend, the government shall have to rethink its service delivery framework through the establishment of a functional State Capacity-Decen-tralization-Service Delivery nexus. This nexus shall only be possible through a re-structuring of the State and a re-examination of its role in the socio-economic development efforts. To achieve this, I propose the following course of action:

First, the number of line ministries at the national level need to be reduced and streamlined. As I mentioned in chapter two, the multiplicity of line ministries has not in any manner, shape or form contributed to better service delivery or enhanced civil service performance. Rather, it has led to cacophony and dupli-cation of responsibilities among line ministries and between line ministries, para-statal agencies, Commissions and Secretariats. Earlier in this chapter I proposed the setting up of properly elected regional governments headed by Governors elected through direct universal suffrage, and accorded full con-stitutional executive authority to freely govern their regions. To that end the Governor shall be the head of a Regional Executive Committee composed of Regional Ministers appointed by him/her. In order to make service delivery more responsive, targeted and bottom-up, I shall further propose that regional line ministries should be directly aligned, in nomenclature and in function, to those of the Central Government. In the same way, the technical departments within the Central Government line ministries shall be aligned to those of the regional ministries. Except that while the technical departments at the national level shall be known as "Directorates" headed by "Directors", those in the regional ministries shall be known as "Divisions" to be headed by "Division Heads".

In this re-structured format, the role of the Central Government line ministries shall be more strategic i.e., policy formulation, planning, program design, coordination, oversight, defining and ensuring compliance with norms and standards. The regional line ministries on their part shall play a more operational role: implementation of national policies and programs, execution of projects, direct service delivery etc.

The ultimate goal of this re-structuring should be to make of the Central Government an enabling by-stander, providing strategic guidance and oversight over the regional governments. As operational agencies, the regional governments shall become the main service providers and executors of national policies and programs. I know questions and fears shall be raised about lack of, or limited technical and institutional capacity of regional governments to fully take up this operational role. I personally believe some of these fears are exaggerated and are sometimes spread by the Yaoundé ruling elite keen on maintaining their power and influence at the center. During the one decade I served in the Cameroon Civil Service, I was fortunate to meet and work with well-trained, dedicated and professionally savvy civil servants serving at regional and divisional levels. The bulk of them were educated at home in Cameroon but had also undergone specialized training in other countries abroad. I met education managers trained at the University Reading in England; environmentalists and agro-economists trained in Israel; development specialists trained in the Netherlands; tax policy experts trained in the US; healthcare professionals public health managers trained in different European and African countries; urban planning engineers trained in China. Yet, some of these people were under-employed and were never really given any opportunity to fully put their expertise at the service of the nation. This was either because they did not have godfathers in Yaoundé to recommend them for appointment to positions best suited to their skills and competences or because they were not vocal militants of the ruling party, which seemed to be the only criterion for appointment to positions of responsibility during the crazy decade that followed the return to multiparty politics.

I experienced this firsthand. After working as a mid-level civil servant for a decade, I obtained a World Bank scholarship to pursue advanced studies at Harvard University. When I returned to Cameroon with a Master's degree in Public Administration (with concentrations in Policy Analysis, Strategic Planning and Political Economy and Development) I was assigned as Economic Adviser to a provincial governor. After three months in the position the only meaningful assignment I carried out was to certify, on behalf of the Governor, the completion of a contract for the construction of classrooms in a Government

Primary School located some thirty kilometers outside of the provincial capital city. It was this sheer waste of my skills and competences that finally led me to request for a temporary cessation of service. I ultimately left the civil service altogether to pursue my career somewhere else and put my professional training at the service of those that needed and valued it the most.

The point I am making is that there is an abundance of trained and competent human resources in the regions capable of making regional governments fully functional and operational. One deleterious effect of Cameroon's highly centralized system is that it stifles the creative and innovative spirit of mid and lower-level civil servants. I believe that the state's capacity for service delivery shall be enhanced if public managers at regional levels are afforded the space to develop and explore their creative energies and direct them towards finding innovative solutions to everyday problems.

This brings me to my second point: establishing synergies between the state and society in all its organized forms and the private sector for enhanced service delivery.

During the colonial period and for about the first two decades after independence in most of Anglophone Cameroon, socio-economic development initiatives were essentially community-driven, with minimal government involvement. The Ring Road in the North-West Region best illustrates this.

The Bamenda Ring Road is a road network that goes from Bamenda to Ndop, to Kumbo, to Nkambe, to Wum and back to Bamenda, thereby "ringing" as it were, the main chief towns of the region, except Fundong and Mbengwi. Most people may not know this but the fact of the matter is that the Ring Road was never consciously or deliberately designed and built as part of a government infrastructure development program. It grew out of the desire of different communities to link their villages to each other for the purposes of trade, person-to-person contacts and other forms of socio-cultural exchanges. To achieve this goal, the communities organized community labor and dug their section of the road up to the boundary with the next village; the next village would take the relay and extend the road to their boundaries with the next village and so on and so forth. The communities worked with mainly rudimentary hand tools. Since they lacked the equipment and proper technology to build bridges, they did the best they could to avoid waterways. That explains in part why most of the road winds dangerously over hill tops.

I have often spoken of the Bamenda Ring Road as the perfect metaphor for, and a concrete exemplification of, needs-based, community-driven development. It speaks to the self-reliant development spirit of a people. Socio-economic development initiatives and grassroots service delivery in Anglophone Cameroon, was a concerted effort between the Native Authority/Area and Clan Councils, the communities and faith-based voluntary organizations.

Take education and health, for instance.

Traditional Rulers (in their capacity as Heads of Native Administrations) welcomed religious organizations to their communities, allocated to them land and protected their rights over those lands. In turn, the religious bodies not only built churches but also provided the communities with schools and hospitals. For most of the colonial period and for decades after independence, the health and education needs of vast majorities of populations in Anglophone Cameroon were taken care of by faith-based organizations attached to the Catholic, Basel Mission (later the Presbyterian Church in Cameroon) and the Cameroon Baptist Convention. Some of the region's most prestigious academic institutions are still faith-based: CPC Bali, Sacred Heart College, St. Joseph's College, Sasse, PSS Kumba, Baptist High School, Queen of Rosary, PSS Batibo, Saker Baptist College, St Paul's Technical College, Joseph Merrick Baptist College etc.

Similarly, healthcare delivery has been in the hands of Mission hospitals like Presbyterian General Hospital Achu Tugi, Mount Mary Hospital in Buea, Presbyterian Hospital Manyemen, Shisong General Hospital, Banso Baptist Hospital, Mbingo Baptist Hospital and leper colony etc. These hospitals have been pacesetters in quality healthcare delivery in the region.

These educational institutions and health facilities went a long way to raise standards of living in these communities. The presence of these facilities also led to the establishment of a nascent cash economy to serve the schools and the hospitals.

This partnership between local authorities, communities and the churches was not only limited to health, education and infrastructure. It extended to the economic and financial sectors. In 1963 a Roman Catholic Priest established the first ever cooperative credit union scheme in Njinikom and later in Nso. By 1967, there were about thirteen registered credit union societies operating mainly around Njinikom and the Nso areas of the Bamenda Grassfields. In 1968, the primary societies came together to form the West Cameroon Credit Union League. The league became a registered member of the African Cooperative Savings and Credit Association. It benefitted from considerable external funding and technical assistance that enabled it to expand out of the Bamenda Grass-fields where it had originally started into the Coastal Regions of the now South West Region. According to the World Council of Credit Unions (WOCCU), the Cameroon Credit Union League, is currently the largest credit union and micro-finance network in Cameroon. As at 2010 its combined membership was 336,187 people with US$240 million in assets.[15] The Cameroon Credit Union system, a private, community initiative, has largely operated independently even though over the years government oversight and supervision have become more intrusive.

It is not always communities and faith-based organizations that come together to gab-fill when the government is unable or unwilling to deliver essential services to its people. At times it is individual citizens who step in to play that role. A plausible example is the creation of the Yaoundé Parents National Education Union (PNEU) School and the General Certificate of Education Board.

The dismantling of the federation and the creation of the Unitary State in 1972, saw an influx of West Cameroonian politicians and civil servants into Yaoundé. They were coming to serve in the new political and administrative institutions of the newly-minted unitary state. Among them was Hon Madame Gwendolyn Burnley. Mme Gwen Burnley was an educationist, career senior civil servant and a rising star of West Cameroon politics. In 1973, she transferred to Yaoundé to serve as a Member of Parliament in the newly constituted National Assembly of the United Republic of Cameroon. Like most West Cameroonians arriving in Yaoundé at the time she was soon faced with the teething problem of the lack of appropriate educational establishments for her young children. In 1973, there were hardly any elementary schools in Yaoundé that catered for the needs of the Anglophone children. Undaunted, Hon Gwen Burnley, like the astute educationist she was, started a home-schooling program for her children in her living room. Soon, other Anglophone parents faced with a similar predicament, started dropping off their kids at her house for schooling. Within a very short time, her living room became too small to accommodate the kids and the home school was moved to the garage of Dr Gothlieb Monekoso. Dr Monekoso was serving at the Faculty of Medicine of the University of Yaoundé at the time. He would go on to become the WHO Regional Director for Africa and Minister of Public Health. As the enrolment continued to rise, the need to create a proper school became imperative. That is how in 1977, under Hon Gwen Burnely's leadership, sixteen Anglophone families came together to create the Parents National Education Union (PNEU) school in Yaoundé. They contributed money, bought a piece of land at the Etoug-Egbe neighborhood and build their

---

15   Jennifer Ballweg, "Cameroon CUs Overcoming Challenges, Growing Membership', WOCCU Press Release, April 2011.

school campus. The PNEU school system is modelled along the home schools that were created by British expatriates in Southern/West Cameroon during the colonial and immediate post-colonial period. It is purely an initiative of the parents, created and managed by them. The parents define the pedagogic and disciplinary standards, limit class sizes, recruit and pay teachers based on a pre-established profile endorsed by its board of directors. Apart from Yaoundé, PNEU schools also exist in Bamenda, Limbe and Douala. The PNEU schools are amongst the most prestigious elementary schools in Cameroon, graduating high achieving children year in year out. I am in the habit of describing the PNEU schools as the jewel on the crown of the Anglophone Education Sub-System. Yet, it was and still is an innovation of parents with very little government input.

In 1991 and 1992, the Cameroon General Certificate of Education (GCE) examinations witnessed a near scandalous drop in standards. The management of the examination process had become very lax, resulting in large scale leakages of question papers. In 1992 the leakages were so widespread and so outrageous that question papers were being openly sold in the streets. In Bamenda town, candidates were known to congregate at a spot on Che Street to purchase question papers every evening. Apart from the leakage of exams question papers, the translation of the questions from French to English left much to be desired, especially at the *Certificat d'Aptitude Professionnel* (CAP), the end of course official exams for the first cycle of technical education at the secondary level. A question in the Motor Mechanics paper read thus: *What is the role of a candle in a motor?* This was obviously a word for word translation of the French version: *Quel est le role des bougies dans un moteur?* Someone in the Education Ministry had translated *"bougie"* as *"candle"* instead of *"plugs"* and *"moteur"* as *"motor"* instead of *"engine"*. The correct English version of the question was supposed to be: *What is the role of heater plugs in an engine?* Needless to say that as a result of this mistranslation Anglophone candidates failed in their numbers. The Ministry of Education (which ran the exams) showed characteristic indifference and nonchalance towards these scandalous leakages and faulty translations that were undermining the integrity of the exams and the certificates issued therefrom. The government seemed totally unfazed and unperturbed by the fact that the lack of integrity in the exams was comprising the future of young Cameroonians.

It was then that the teachers and the parents stepped in to redeem what remained of the prestige of the GCE as an examination and to forestall its rapid decline. The teachers, grouped under the Teachers Association of Cameroon (TAC) and the parents, working as a Confederation of Parents Teacher Associations, came together to pressure the Government to create an examination board.

In doing so, they argued that the Department of Examinations in the Ministry of Education had proven itself incapable of organizing high stake testing. And that responsibility needed to be delegated to a competent specialized technical body, like an independent examinations board. In that regard they recommended the creation of a Cameroon Examination Board, which should henceforth be responsible for organizing official examinations from end to end in the country. True to type the government was having none of it. The Minister of Education argued at the time that national examinations was a matter of national sovereignty and so the government could not delegate it to another agency. A tug of war ensued between the Minister on the one hand and the parents and teachers on the other. In the end the government caved in and two examination boards were created: one for the GCE and another for the Baccalaureate.

Communities have also been at the forefront of catering for their own potable water supply needs. In most of Anglophone Cameroon the first water projects were community-owned and community managed – like in Bali and Kumbo. Some of these community water schemes have since broken down after government decided that water systems should be run by state concessionaries in urban areas and by city and municipal councils in urban and semi-urban areas.

The above examples serve to show that in matters of service delivery there are areas where communities, citizen initiative groups and decentralized government institutions have a comparative advantage over the State/Central Government. Empirical research has shown that collaborative partnerships for enhance service delivery between state, civil society and communities work better at decentralized and subnational levels of the State.[16] Oftentimes, when left to themselves, communities have done a better job at diagnosing their problems and seeking the best ways to sustainably address them. But they must be afforded the space to freely do so. I believe that space best exists within regional and local government structures directly elected by the people and answerable to the people. The capacity of the Cameroon State to promote broad-based socio-economic development and achieve the objectives set out in Cameroon Vision 2035 shall largely depend on how it implements its current decentralization process and how Regional and Local Authorities shall be positioned and purposed for enhanced service delivery. Shall the Central Government (the State) accept the role of an enabling bystander and allow the regions and councils to take up greater responsibilities in service delivery? Given the proclivity of Cameroon's ruling elite towards centralized authority, I doubt this shall ever happen.

16   See Tendler, J. (1997). *Good Government in the Tropics*: Johns Hopkins University Press.

Nevertheless, quite clearly the government's options are limited here. The present top-down, centralized approach to governance and to service delivery have clearly shown its limits. It has proven itself incapable of providing the impetus needed to move the country forward. But as I have shown in this chapter, a well-thought-out decentralization process, implemented with good faith and strong political will, can constitute a viable starting point for the re-structuring and the refoundation of this country in a manner consistent with the promise of its founding. If the current ruling class is truly looking to keep this country one and indivisible, or to make it an emerging economy by 2035, then it should embrace decentralization, not fear it.

Decentralization alone, no matter how well intentioned, shall not be enough to transform a country as complex as Cameroon. It shall have to be accompanied and complemented by profound public service reform. In the next chapter, I discuss the urgent need for rethinking this country's public service delivery model. And it should be a model capable of transforming this country into a modern progressive state, dedicated to social service, as its founders had envisioned.

Chapter Four

The Imperative of Public Service Reform

In a very broad sense "Public Service" is the term used to describe a wide range of services that a government is normally expected to provide to its population. Such services normally include things like quality healthcare and education, safety and security, safe drinking water, food, decent housing, guarantees for old age pensions, employment, infrastructure etc. These services can be provided directly through public corporations or indirectly through private initiatives funded by the government. The provision of public services is the ultimate function and raison d'etre of government. It is the basis of the exercise of state power.

Public Service Delivery and State Authority

Leon Deguit, a leading French scholar of Public Law, stresses that the continuous and uninterrupted provision of public service is what underpins the exercise of state authority. In his very instructive essay "The Concept of Public Service" Deguit defines public service as:

> Every activity of general interest which is of such an importance to the entire collectivity that those in authority are under a duty to insure its accomplishment in an absolutely continuous manner, even by the use of force.[1]

Deguit sees and understands the role of the state, not in terms of its power or its absolute sovereignty, but it terms of its ability to leverage public service delivery and the obligation of those in authority to ensure this happens. In that regard, Deguit affirms that:

---

1   Duguit, L. (1923). The Concept of Public Service. *Yale Law Journal, 32*(5). P.431

> The state thus ceases to be a sovereign power which commands. It is a cooperation of public services, constituted, regulated, directed, and controlled by those in authority, who in doing so fulfill the obligation imposed upon them by the rule of law based upon the social solidarity. [2]

Deguit's definition of public service is very relevant to this treatise because it establishes a near metaphysical nexus between the State and Service Provision. In a very poignant way, it reminds those who exercise any form of governmental authority to make of the continuous and uninterrupted provision of public service to the citizenry an obligation. Such a reminder is important in a country like Cameroon where citizens have come to expect nothing from their government, except maybe, a hard time. In Cameroon, public service delivery is no longer a right. It is considered as some sort of a favor from the government to its people and for which the people are supposed to show gratitude through marches and motions of support.

This is quite simply an aberration that needs to be fixed. The refoundation of this nation shall therefore require near revolutionary reforms in public service provisioning.

Early Attempts at Public Service Reform

Attempts at a meaningful, coordinated and well thought-out public service reform in Cameroon have been somewhat perfunctory, since unification. The emphasis has always been on "administrative reform" understood as "civil service reform". In the early days of the Republic, a state agency, the General Inspectorate of Administrative Reform (better known by its French acronym IGERA) was set up to oversee administrative and civil service reform across line ministries. In 1988, President Biya dissolved IGERA and created the Ministry of Public Service, Administrative Reform and State Control. In 1994 a separate ministry in charge of State Control was created and attached to the President's Office.

It is important to underline here the important conceptual differences between the "public service" and the "civil service" in French and in English. In Cameroon, "public service" is usually translated into French as "fonction publique", which in effect is "civil service" in English. So the notion of "public service' is often conflated with the "civil service". The civil service is the government administrative apparatus (especially the human resource part of it) responsible for delivering public services. Broadly speaking public service reform is about

2   ibid

improving the way governments perform, with regard to its ability to deliver services to its population. Civil Service reform is about enhancing the performance of government employees for public service delivery.

Administrative Reforms Post-Ahidjo

For most of his twenty-two years in power, President Ahmadou Ahidjo mostly worked with the public service delivery model he inherited from the French colonial government. It was basically a centralized, top-down, state-centric model with very little citizens' voice and participation. However, within the framework of the five-year development planning model, Development Committees were set up at Provincial and Divisional levels in 1977. These committees were intended to serve as grassroots participatory fora where local development priorities were discussed and adopted for inclusion into the Five Year Development Plan. But it never went deep enough. The committees met at Provincial and Divisional capitals and mostly brought together the political and administrative elite of the Province or the Division. Quite often, it was more of an information-sharing session where the Delegate for Plan and Regional Development presented to the participants for their endorsement, a list of projects already programmed by the Central Government. That notwithstanding, under Ahidjo's authoritarian rule, corruption and administrative laxity were minimal and things got done. Some of the great educational institutions and professional schools, health facilities, roads, airports, urban pipe borne water systems, sports and recreational infrastructure, which propelled Cameroon into the status of a lower middle income economy, were built at this time.

On his part, President Biya came to power in 1982 promising administrative and government reform. He was a career civil service bureaucrat with a reputation for hard work. In his first ever inaugural address as Head of State he decried the crippling effects of administrative bottlenecks on government performance. He declared the dawn of a new era: the era of the New Deal, marked by rigor and moralization in the management of public affairs. Three months after taking office, the President paid his first visit outside the national capital to Bamenda where he promised to put an end to the costly trips made to the capital, Yaoundé, for the purpose of chasing files. It was obvious that the new President's priority was going to be administrative and government reform. Not political reforms.

Soon after taking over office, Mr. Biya was locked in a ruthless, internecine political battle with his predecessor, Mr. Ahmadou Ahidjo. Soldiers loyal to Mr. Ahidjo tried to overthrow Mr. Biya in a coup d'état in April 1984, barely seventeen months into his presidency. As the fight between the two men raged on, Mr. Biya's focus shifted away from administrative reform to political maneuvering. By 1985 he had succeeded to politically neutralize Ahmadou Ahidjo and so, he turned his attention back to administrative and government reform.

In this regard, the President set up a high-powered fact-finding commission composed of senior officials of the government and his ruling CPDM party, headed by one of his senior aides, Joseph Zambo.

The Zambo Commission

The Commission, which came to be known as the Zambo Commission, was tasked to tour the country and solicit ideas and proposals from the grassroots on how to improve government and civil service performance. The Commission visited all the ten provinces of the country, holding broad based consultative meetings at each stop. From North to South and from East to West, the people were very consistent in their demands: greater administrative decentralization. The Zambo Commission, in its report, made far-reaching recommendations, which if dutifully implemented, could have been the first real and conscious effort at public and civil service reform since independence. As far as I recall, the only key action that was taken on the recommendations of the Zambo Commission was the harmonization of official civil service working hours.

Before the Zambo Commission there were two different official civil service working hours in Cameroon, one for the Francophone part of the country and another for the Anglophone part of the country. The Francophone regions operated a two shift system (morning and afternoons with a two and a half hour break from 12:20 pm), Mondays to Fridays, and half day of work (from 8 am to 1 pm) on Saturdays. In the Anglophone regions the working week went from Monday to Friday, with a single shift which went from 7:30 am to 3:30 am daily, with no work on Saturdays. The Zambo Commission argued that the two-shift system was too costly to civil servants in the Francophone zone as they had to commute to and from work at least four times a day, thus making them less productive. Additionally, the Commission also contended that going to work on Saturdays, even for half a day, left the civil servants with very little free time they may need to do other things like engaging in agriculture. The Zambo Commission thus recommended the uniformisation of working hours all over the national territory. Hence, official working hours went from 8 am to 4 pm, Mondays through Fridays with no work on Saturdays.

The Economic Crisis and Government Reform

The economic crisis that hit the country in1985 elicited new calls for pro-found institutional and public service reforms, this time led by international finance institutions, notably the World Bank and the International Monetary Fund, as part of the Structural Adjustment Program. In line with the core prin-ciples of the Washington Consensus and in true Bretton Woods institutions tradition, Structural Adjustment came with strict conditionalities that were supposedly intended to lead to macro-economic stabilization and greater eco-nomic liberalization. In this regard, the conditionalities called for an overhaul of the financial governance system (notably, taxation, customs and excise, and budget management), privatization of state owned enterprises, the lifting of trade barriers and barriers to foreign investment, the institution of fiscal discipline and a reduction in public expenditure.

In the late eighties and early nineties, Structural Adjustment was a conten-tious issue in Africa, due largely to the hardship it imposed on the population. Privatization of state-owned enterprises and reduction of the government work-force meant massive retrenchments and job losses, which in turn could spark popular discontent. The early nineties was also a period of political turmoil engendered by the return to multi-party politics. The political status quo was being challenged by the nascent opposition parties and pressure groups, and the once powerful autocracy found itself literally fighting for its own political survival. So, when it came to implementing the reforms recommended by the SAP, the government chose to tread cautiously. It bowed to pressure to cut civil service salaries and retrench a part of the government workforce as part of the measures to reduce public expenditure. Some state-owned enterprises were also liquidated, and a few were privatized, mostly the small and moribund ones. But when it came to the privatization of the larger, more strategic, state-owned enterprises, the government resisted, preferring to increase their performance and productivity through performance contracts.

Different evaluation reports of the World Bank, the International Monetary Fund and the African Development Bank affirm that the reforms implemented under the Structural Adjustment programs did indeed put Cameroon back on the path of economic growth as the country went from negative growth rate in FY 1991/92 to 5 per cent GDP growth in FY 1997/98. However, this seemingly significant improvement in macro-economic performance was not matched by similar improvements in public service delivery.

Global Doctrines of Public Service Reform

In the nineties, two mutually reinforcing and tangentially connected doctrines dominated the global discourse on public service (or government) reform, to wit, New Public Management and Reinventing Government.

The New Public Management Doctrine

In 1991 Christopher Hood (a professor of Public Administration and Public Policy at the University of London) coined the phrase "New Public Management" to describe prior attempts at enhancing the performance and efficiency of public organizations through the use of business-like models. In this regard, New Public Management (or NPM for short) emphasized the need to incorporate private sector models to public service delivery, notably, customer satisfaction, cost-effectiveness, results-oriented, and decentralized decision-making.

Hood summarized the key doctrinal components of NPM in seven precepts, namely: hands-on professional management in the public sector (by which he meant an active, visible. discretionary control of organizations from named persons at the top, 'free to manage"); explicit standards and measures of performance (which he defined in terms of goals, targets, indicators of success, preferably expressed in quantitative terms, especially for professional services); greater emphasis on output controls (resource allocation and rewards linked to measured performance and the breakup of centralized bureaucracy-wide personnel management); shift to disaggregation of units in the public sector (break up of formerly 'monolithic' units; unbundling of U-form management systems into corporatized units around products, operating on decentralized 'one-line' budgets and dealing with one another on an 'arms-length' basis); shift to greater competition in public sector (move to term contracts and public tendering procedures); stress on private sector styles of management practice (move away from military-style public service ethic, greater flexibility in hiring and rewards; greater use of PR techniques); stress on greater discipline and parsimony in resource use (cutting direct costs, raising labor discipline, resisting union demands, limiting 'compliance costs' to business).[3]

The Reinventing Government Concepts

In 1992 David Osborne and Ted Gaebler published their seminal work *Reinventing Government: How the Entrepreneurial Spirit is Transforming the*

---

3   See Hood, C. (1991). A Public Management for All Seasons? *Public Administration, 69*(1), 3-19. pp. 4-5

Public Sector. In the book they argued that the American public service delivery system, which was created during the industrial age and best suited to the needs of the economic and military crises that followed, was no longer relevant to the post-industrial information age.[4] Osborne and Gaebler contended that government in the US had become bureaucratic, sluggish, hierarchically-centralized, rule-based, wasteful and inefficient. Government was said to be so incompetent that it could not even successfully organize a two-car parade. For government to improve on its public service provisioning, it needed to be less bureaucratic and more effective. In this regard, Osborne and Gaebler proposed ten principles for reinventing government so as to make it more entrepreneurial and better performing.

These innovative principles recommended a transformative model for government that was catalytic (steering rather than rowing); community-owned (empowering rather than serving); competitive (injecting competition into service delivery); mission-driven (transforming rules-driven organizations); results-oriented (funding outcomes instead of inputs); customer-driven government (meeting the needs of the customer, not the bureaucracy); enterprising (earning rather than spending); anticipatory (preventing rather than curing); decentralized (based on participation and teamwork, not hierarchies); and market-oriented (leveraging change through the market).

These principles, the authors posited, were expected to bring about a fundamental transformation of public systems and organizations. They were also intended to create dramatic increases in their effectiveness, efficiency, adaptability, and capacity to innovate. Ultimately, reinvention was about making broad and systematic changes in how government administers its programs.[5]

Global Effects of NPM and Reinventing Government

New Public Management and Reinventing Government, as conceptual frameworks, fitted squarely into a growing global movement for public service and government reform, especially in the early nineties. NPM provided the underlying principles and the intellectual basis for public sector reform in Britain, Australia, New Zealand and the OECD countries in general. On its part, reinventing government served as the cornerstone for President Clinton's

---

4   Osborne, D., & Gaebler, T. (1992). *Reinventing government: How the entrepreneurial spirit is transforming the public sector*. New York: Addison-Wesley.

5   Thompson, F. J., & Riccucci, N. M. (1998). Reinventing Government. *Annual Review of Political Science, 1*(1), 231-257.

National Performance Review program launched in 1993.

Overall, the underlying goal of NPM and reinventing government was to advance what came to be known as the three "e"s of the new paradigm for public service delivery, namely, effectiveness (enhancing government's ability to achieve program goals), efficiency (increasing its achievement relative to cost) and economy (slashing its price tag). This is what is at the core of governance. And it is a dynamic best captured in the World Governance Indicators of "government effectiveness". Yet for the past twenty years, Cameroon's performance in that indicator has averaged 20 per cent, well below the Sub Saharan Africa average of 26 per cent

As I mentioned earlier in this chapter, after the outbreak of the economic crisis in Cameroon in 1985, most attempts at public service reform were geared towards meeting the conditionalities that came with the Structural Adjustment Program. So, understandably, these reforms were somewhat circumscribed to the public finance sector. Scanty attention was paid to the overhaul of the social service delivery system. In fact, South Africa and Rwanda (both of whom were emerging from conflict in the mid-nineties) are among the very few African countries that undertook a conscious effort to apply the principles of reinventing government and New Public Management to the public service reform agendas.

The refoundation of the Cameroon nation shall require a complete rethink of how the government delivers services to its population. This will entail a public service reform that is innovative, bold, and assertive and pragmatic, derived from the honest recognition that most of what we have done in the past 60 years in that regard has yielded very little meaningful results. The principles of reinventing government and NPM could serve as useful guides and viable starting points. In this regard I set forth below, suggestions for enhancing public service provisioning based on the criteria enunciated above – innovative, bold, assertive and pragmatic.

An "Enabling" Versus a "Doing" Central Government

Part of the reason why public service delivery in Cameroon is painfully slow, lackluster and perilous is simply because the Central Government is biting more than it can chew. As I noted in the previous chapters, the Central Government manages more than 90 per cent of the public investment projects, with councils and municipalities responsible for less than 10 per cent. It is inconceivable that a Minister can sit in Yaoundé and believe that he or she can oversee the implementation of thousands of projects all over the national territory and do so with any level of effectiveness and timeliness.

Allocative Efficiency in Service Provision

A fundamental principle of decentralization is *allocative efficiency*. This principle holds that service delivery can have better outcomes if the design and implementation of programs and decisions on the allocation of resources are taken at the level, and with the active participation of, the beneficiary community or party. In Cameroon, this has often not been the case. And I have evidence of this.

In 1999, while serving as Divisional Officer (D.O.) for Oku Subdivision, I received a message from the Director of General Administration of the Ministry of Territorial Administration, asking me to come to Yaoundé and collect a set of chairs for my official residence. I found that rather strange because at that time there was no official resident for the D.O of Oku. In fact I was squatting in the official accommodation of the Head of the Elak Integrated Health Center. It was totally confounding to me that someone sat at the headquarters in Yaoundé and decided that what the D.O. of Oku needed most were chairs for a non-existent residence, and then went ahead to procure the kind of chairs he believed would fit into that non-existent residence. Had I been consulted, I would have told the Director, or whoever was taking those insane decisions, what the immediate priorities of the Oku Sub Divisional Office were. And living room chairs were definitely not one of them. I never went to Yaoundé to collect the chairs and I don't know where or how they ended up. Here was a classic instance of allocative inefficiency that obviously led to a waste of resources. And instances like this are fairly routine in Cameroon and they are not limited to the equipping of the residences of Local Administrative Officers. They extend broadly to other critical areas like water supply projects, the location and construction of schools and health facilities etc. I shall come back to this later, especially with regard to schools.

Re-defining Central-Local Roles for Enhanced Public Service Delivery

I believe this anomaly can be corrected through a rethinking and a re-structuring of the functional relationships and a redefinition of roles between the Central Government on the one hand and Regional, City and Municipal Councils, on the other. As I noted in the last chapter, this restructuring and redefinition of roles should result in a new paradigm for public service delivery in which the Central Government becomes an enabling bystander, while the Regional, City and Municipal Councils assume the role of "doers". Or as Osborne and Gaebler put it, the Central Government shall "steer" while the regional councils and municipalities shall "row' the boat of service delivery. This in effect means that the Central Government shall assume a more strategic role: providing leadership and guidance, setting standards and norms, developing policy frameworks and ensuring their compliance. The Regional, City and Municipal Councils on the other hand, shall take up more operational functions: hands-on delivery of services in critical areas of human development like health and sanitation, education, potable water supply, waste management, environmental management, physical urban planning and development, etc.

To enhance this shared responsibility, I believe the number of line Ministries need to be streamlined and reduced to a maximum of 25 (down from the current 38) and a maximum of 35 ministers of all ranks (down from the current 71). For better efficiency and coordination, Regional Ministries and their directorates should also be closely aligned to those of the Central Government both in name and in nomenclature. Elected Regional Governors exercising full executive authority should be empowered to lead the public service delivery programs in their respective regions.

One area I believe this new paradigm for service delivery can work is in education.

The Example of the Education Sector

Before independence, education was largely in the hands of faith-based organizations, notably the Catholic and Protestant churches, who undertook the critical tasks of training teachers, building and running schools. There are three main requisites for a school: a curriculum, a faculty, and facilities. In other words, for an institution to be considered a place of learning (or a school) it must have a teaching program or syllabus (curriculum) that is being dispensed by qualified teachers (a faculty) in an environment set aside for this purpose with adequate and adapted infrastructure (facilities). Examples of educational facilities include: classrooms, playgrounds, a sick bay, a library, toilets, canteen, gymnasium and an auditorium. The missionaries strictly respected these norms when setting up their schools and that is why, to these day, mission schools, especially the secondary schools, are still among the best and the most prestigious institutions of learning in this country. When government started creating and building secondary schools after independence, it followed the example of the missionary schools, and made sure educational establishments at all levels respected those three norms. That explains why most of the secondary schools built immediately after independence and unification and those built under the five-year development plan were well-planned and imbued with the prestige and aura of respectable educational institutions.

All this was to change from 1990 onwards, when the ruling Cameroon People's Democratic Movement party was fighting an epic existential battle, engendered by stiff challenges to its hegemony emanating from the emerging and rapidly growing political opposition. In a bid to leverage support and compensate party followers for their loyalty, the government began randomly creating schools, both primary and secondary, and awarding contracts for their construction to its supporters. Quite often, the schools were created without any consultations with the beneficiary community as to where they were to be built. The creation of schools was no longer intended as a means of expanding access to education but rather as a political gambit intended to compensate party loyalists. The results are what we see today. At best, government schools in Cameroon, especially those built after 1990, look like bus stations and at worse, like prison yards. They often lack basic facilities like toilets and running water, sick bays, playgrounds, gymnasiums. Administrative and staff offices and libraries are often lacking and far-fetched. The idea of a properly planned "school campus", once the norm in Cameroon, doesn't seem to be the case anymore. However, a Senior Adviser in the Ministry of Basic Education holds that, in its efforts to expand access to basic education, the government has adopted basic norms for "mass education schools". These norms include a standard classroom, a playground and at least a teacher per classroom.

As I noted in chapter two, educational outcomes and the quality of learning at the primary level in Cameroon, especially in public schools and in rural areas, continue to be poor in spite of substantial increases in the number of schools built, the number of teachers trained and deployed and the budget allocation to the education sector. There is no doubt in my mind that this sordid and inauspicious state of affairs shall persist until Cameroon adopts a bold and innovative operational framework for delivering quality education to its children in an effective and efficient manner. Such a framework must be decentralized and team-based, in accordance with the principles of the General Code of Regional and Local Authorities. In this regard, I believe that the operational framework that can best serve this purpose is the School District system.

School District System

School Districts are decentralized corporate-like bodies charged with the delivery of elementary and secondary education within a public education system. In the U.S some of the core responsibilities of a School District include:
   * Selecting curriculum materials (textbooks, films, etc.)
   * Assigning, hiring, and dismissing staff (teachers, principals, secretaries,

counselors, etc.)
* Monitoring finances and ensuring budget requirements are met; choosing how to spend funds
* Ensuring that all activities of the schools in the area comply with state and federal laws, such as those dealing with the length of the school day, school lunches, special education facilities, and more.
* Keeping track of, maintaining, and supplying the school buildings with necessary equipment such as computers, physical education equipment.
* Ensuring safety and security of schools. [6]

In South Africa, the Ministry of Basic Education assigns to the School District the responsibility of working *"collaboratively with principals and educators in schools ....to improve educational access and retention, give management and professional support, and help schools achieve excellence in learning and teaching"*. In this regard the education districts have been assigned four main roles, namely:
* Planning
* Support
* Oversight
* Accountability and Public Engagement. [7]

Some of these core functions of a School District are already provided for in the General Code of Regional and Local Authorities. Section 271 of the General Code mandates the Regional Councils to create, equip, manage and maintain government secondary and high schools as well as colleges within its area of responsibility. The Regional Council is also given the task of recruiting and managing teaching and support staff of such institutions. I strongly recommend to the Regional Councils, to borrow a leaf from their South African and US counterparts, and take the bold and innovative step of creating School Districts and positioning them as decentralized operational mechanisms for delivering quality education to a burgeoning youthful population. It is also in the interest of the Central Government to encourage and support Regional Councils to take such bold and innovative initiatives, without which it shall be difficult to achieve the education objectives set out in the Cameroon Vision 2035 and the SDGs.

---

6   As per Jeffrey Johnson, "What are the Powers and Duties of a School District?", December 2019
7   Culled from the website of the South African Ministry of Basic Education. https://www.education.gov.za/Informationfor/EducationDistricts.aspx

Review of School Management Boards

I am aware that since the 1990s there have been attempts by the National Ministries in charge of Education to create holistic, community-based approaches to the management of schools. School Management Boards, comprised of different education stakeholders within the school community, were set up to serve as a strategic forum for overseeing the implementation of government policy and the defense of community interests in the schools. But like with anything else in Cameroon in the 1990s, this well-intentioned project was soon hijacked by politicians. In Momo Division, where I was serving at the time as First Assistant Senior Divisional Officer, most of the School Board Chairpersons appointed by the Minister were prominent members of the ruling CPDM party. In a Division that was predominantly opposition, the creation of school boards and the appointment of their chairpersons based on political considerations became a very contentious issue. And as can be expected, the school boards never really took off.

The government learnt from this debacle and tried to remedy things. In 2001 the School Boards were replaced by School Councils. Members of the School Council are drawn from what a Senior Adviser in the Ministry of Basic Education calls the "education community" and the "active forces of the community".[8] The executive members of the school's Parents Teacher Association are also members. The School Council is intended to play the same role as that of the Board of Directors of a State-owned Enterprise. Unlike the School Boards, the chairperson of the School Council is elected, not appointed. However, the School Councils have been unable to effectively take off; its statutes are once more being revised, according to the Senior Adviser.

Empowered and adequately resourced School Districts, reporting to and being overseen by, properly constituted Education Boards, should be able to resolve some of these teething technical and management issues that are undermining the effective and efficient delivery of public education to the nation's children. The General Code of Regional and Local Councils already provides the framework for this. It is time for the Central Government to stand back and allow the regions and their strategic partners (like the churches, lay private school proprietors, the teachers, the parents and the communities) to take on a more operational role in the education of our youths – as they were doing long before the Central Government got involved.

But the creation of school districts alone cannot guarantee better educational

---

8   As per Mr Tohmoh Joseph, Technical Adviser No 2 in the Ministry of Basic Education.

outcomes. It has to be accompanied by profound reforms in the other areas like teacher training, pedagogic inspection and safety and security in schools.

Teacher Training Reform

There are two teaching corps in Cameroon: one for teachers of nursery and elementary education (categorized as B1 and B2) and another for secondary education (categorized as A1 for teachers of 1st cycle of secondary (grammar, technical and commercial) category A2 for teachers of 2nd cycle secondary (grammar, technical and commercial) education.

Nursery and elementary school teachers are trained in Teacher Training Colleges. The basic entry requirement is GCE advanced or Ordinary levels and the duration of the training ranges from one to three years depending on the basic entry qualification. Upon graduation they are awarded the Teacher Grade 1 Certificate. There are separate Teacher Training Colleges for general education, and for technical and commercial education. Grade 1 teachers are absorbed in the Civil Service at Category B1 and can progressively rise to B2.

First cycle secondary school teachers are trained in the Higher Teacher Training Colleges, where the basic academic entry requirement is GCE Advanced Level. The training is generally subject-specific and lasts for three years. Upon graduation, candidates are awarded the Diploma in Secondary Education Cycle 1 and absorbed into the civil service at category A1. Second cycle secondary school teachers are also trained in the 2nd cycle of the Higher Teacher Training Colleges. Basic academic entry requirement is a first degree and the training lasts for two years. At the end of the course, candidates are awarded the Diploma in Secondary Education Cycle 2 and are absorbed into the Civil Service at Category A2. There are separate training schools for teachers of general education and those of technical and commercial education.

As can be readily seen, the teaching corps in Cameroon is administratively and professionally hierarchical thus creating the impression of 'inferior' teachers at the elementary level and 'superior' teachers at secondary level. This overt discrimination within one of the most essential professional corps in the country has persisted since independence. It does not bode well for the moral of teachers. Such an archaic and outmoded system of categorization needs to be reformed if the country hopes to achieve its long term educational goals.

Within the context of the refoundation of this nation, I am proposing a bold reform of teacher training aimed at the uniformisation of training and professional categories.

The teaching corps in Cameroon needs to be uniformized and delayered.

And this starts with training. I recommend the abolishing of the Teacher Training Colleges and the Grade 1 teachers corps. In the same line I recommend the transformation of all the existing Higher Teacher Training Colleges into full-fledged Schools of Education offering, associate degrees, bachelor's degree, master's degree and doctorate degree programs in Education. Basic academic entry requirement to a three-year bachelor of education program shall be the Advanced Level. During the third year, or maybe sometimes during their training, students shall be asked to specialize in one of the following core areas: Early Childhood Education, Elementary Education or Secondary Education (with a subject-specific stream), among others. It would be understood that those who specialize in early childhood education shall be deployed to nursery schools; those who specialize in elementary education shall be sent to primary schools and those who chose secondary education shall be expected to serve in secondary schools. The teachers shall be absorbed into the Civil Service at Category (B1 for holders of associate degrees) A1 for holders of a Bachelor Degree and at Category A2 for holders of Master's Degree and above. Such changes shall ensure there are qualified teachers at all levels of the educational system. Furthermore, the inferiority and superiority complexes that now exist within the teaching corps should cease to exist, therefore boosting morale among teachers. But if the government chooses to maintain the Grade 1 Teacher Corps, I suggest that an above average competency in mathematics be instituted as a core entry and end-of-course certification requirement. This should help address the gaps identified in the 2019 PASEC assessment of teacher competences in mathematics.

Pedagogic Inspection

These proposed reforms in teacher training and professional categorization need to be accompanied by further reforms in pedagogic or education inspection. Ideally, Pedagogic Inspectors are supposed to be a team of seasoned educators offering guidance to colleagues in the classroom, helping to develop innovative methods of teaching and learning that can best enhance the classroom experience so as to achieve better educational outcomes. This demands specialized skills and profiles that are not readily discernible through an "appointment" system. Pedagogic Inspectors are appointed from within the teaching corps without any set criteria. I know of a teacher who really didn't like teaching because she was never good at it. Then she went to the Ministry of Education and lobbied to be appointed a Provincial Pedagogic Inspector. And she was. So today, we have an incompetent teacher who never liked teaching in the first place, supervising the work of other teachers in the classroom. And this is the kind of person who is expected to mentor, guide and coach teachers and help them overcome their everyday challenges in the classroom. This may be an isolated case but it is still something that need not be happening. I am therefore proposing a system whereby prospective Pedagogic Inspectors shall be expected to undergo specialized training after a minimum of ten years of classroom experience. The specialized training should be followed by a qualification test and accreditation before they are appointed to that position.

Safety and Security in Schools

Another area that requires rethinking is the question of safety and security in the nation's schools, especially the public schools. Of recent there have been recurrent cases of violent conduct, sometimes occasioning death in some of the nation's public schools. In Yaoundé, a student reportedly stabbed a teacher to death in a public school and another student reportedly stabbed a fellow student to death in a Douala school. Drug use, violent crimes and sexual immorality are known to be rampant in the nation's schools as well. But somehow the government doesn't seem to be taking measures to respond to these rapid but nefarious changes in the school environment. The emphasis is still very much on discipline, not safety and security. Senior Discipline Masters are not equipped to deal with the kind of violence we see in our schools these days, some of which often involve the use of drugs, firearms and bladed weapons. There is the overwhelming need to shift the emphasis from "Discipline" to "Safety and Security". Discipline is about the conduct of individual staff and students. Safety and Security is about creating a safe and secure environment for teaching and learning to take place; an environment free of violence. In this regard, I am proposing the establishment of a School Marshal System. School Marshalls, well trained on how to deal with young people, should be equipped and assign to schools. Their mission shall be to work with the school management and parents to enforce the code of conduct for the school and ensure the safety and security of learners, staff and school property.

These are some of the areas of education reform on which I think the Central Government can define policy, set standards and norms, stand back and oversee their implementation by Regional Councils and School Districts.

Harnessing and Leveraging Civic Entrepreneurship

The Kumbo Water Supply Imbroglio

In 2011, the Government issued a number of executive orders transferring some of the Central Government's responsibilities to councils. The responsibility for the supply of safe drinking water to the population in semi-urban and rural areas was thus ceded to councils. In Kumbo, chief town of Bui Division, this transfer sparked an internecine conflict between the Kumbo Water Authority (KWA) and the Governor of the North West Region over what I was made to believe was the refusal of KWA to handover the management of the Kumbo Water Supply system to the Kumbo Urban Council, as demanded in the Prime Minister's executive orders.[9] It is important to note that the people of Kumbo believe that the Kumbo Water Supply Scheme is a community water project. It was built between 1968 and 1970, largely through community effort supported by the Canadian Government, and with financial and technical assistance of the West Cameroon State Government and the Federal Government. For fourteen years (1970 to1984) the water scheme was managed as a community water scheme, under the leadership of the Fon (traditional ruler) of Nso.

In 1984, the government ordered the community to hand over the water scheme to the National Water Corporation (better known by its French acronym SNEC). The people of Kumbo resisted the move but eventually the Kumbo Water project was handed over to SNEC, a government subsidiary. It is said that when SNEC took over, the water supply standards fell while water rates rose. Public water taps were shut down by the corporation for non-payment of bills and the people, unable to access the relatively safe public drinking water, resorted to fetching water from unsafe streams.[10] This obviously caused a lot of resentment within the population who strongly believed that the government and SNEC had brazenly 'stolen' their water project. In 1991, as the political turmoil engendered by the return to multiparty politics raged in the North West Province, the people of Kumbo successfully chased away SNEC and took back control of their water scheme. They created a new organization to manage it: the Kumbo Water Authority. The Government has again asked KWA to handover the Kumbo Water Scheme to the Kumbo Urban Council, as part of transfer of competences from Central Government to municipal councils, within the purview of decentralization.

The fact of the matter is that for most of the colonial and immediate post-independence period, communities did a better job building and managing their own water schemes. Government came into the business of building and

---

9   Those orders had been issued within the framework of the implementation of the Decen-
    tralization Law of 2004
10   Page, B. (2003). Communities as the agents of commodification: The Kumbo Water Authority
     in Northwest Cameroon. *Geoforum, 34*(4), 483-498. p.488

managing water projects much later. And truth be told, most of the government-sponsored, small scale, community-level water projects of the 1970s and 1980s failed woefully. A good example is the SCANWATER projects.

The SCANWATER project was a rural community water scheme implemented in several Cameroonian villages between the 1970s and the early 1990s. It consisted of drilling a borehole, installing a submersible pump in it, then using a diesel-powered generator to pump the water up to an overhead reservoir and then into the community. As a rural community water scheme, the SCANWATER projects were ill-adapted. Because of the high cost of diesel, the communities were unable to run the generators. In addition, the cost of maintaining the equipment and of treating the water turned out to be prohibitively high for the communities. By the early 1990s, the scheme had all but collapsed. Most communities replaced it with the "water-by-gravity" schemes which were cheaper to build and to maintain.

That is why I am at a loss to understand the government's highhanded and arm-twisting approach to the current ruckus between the KWA and KUC over the management of the Kumbo water scheme. It is clear that KWA has better experience and benefits from a high level of community trust than KUC, when it comes to the management of its water supply. So it is baffling to me why the government should seek confrontation not compromise.

Perceived Government aversion towards Citizen Engagement in Service Delivery

Historically the Cameroon government's default attitude towards citizens, communities, or voluntary organizations taking initiatives to enhance public service delivery has been to block them. It would seem the Government has over the years, developed a visceral and intestinal aversion for any civic or community initiative aimed at improving the quality of life of the population. I am not sure I know why but I suspect that people in government believe that if citizens and communities start taking over control of their lives by by-passing government and taking care of their own needs, it would make them (the government people) become irrelevant. Worst still, it will make them look bad and they could lose control over the citizenry. This could explain why in 1993 the Government fought hard to stop the creation of the Cameroon General Certificate of Education Board, an initiative of Anglophone Cameroon teachers and parents that was intended to improve the conduct and credibility of national exams.

But all this need not be happening if public managers in Cameroon were to learn the benefits of harnessing and leveraging civic entrepreneurship.

Notions of Civic Entrepreneurship and Public Service Provisioning
Authors, Charles Leadbeater and Sue Goss, define civic entrepreneurship as:

> …the renegotiation of the mandate and sense of purpose of a public organization, which allows it to find new ways of combining resources and people, both public and private, to deliver better social outcomes, higher social value and more social capital.[11]

In a 2012 blog post titled "Social Innovation, Community and Civic Entrepreneurship: Are Governments Ready?" Joan Vinyets, affirmed that:

> Transformative social progress is only possible if we take advantage of tacit knowledge, citizen networks, communities of practice, and civic entrepreneurship. What we need is to build relationships across the public, private and civic sectors – promoting civic engagement and community problem solving.[12]

The building of these new relationships of innovative public service provisioning shall require a different, not to say, new, role for government. In that regard, Vinyets again asserts that:

> The challenge to engage civic entrepreneurs requires governments to embrace and develop a new role regarding the social services (health, education, etc.,) beyond the means of production. They need to focus on how to leverage and facilitate the production of value, how to sett [sic] up systems to ensure quality outcomes, and to push the bounds of how to address public problems in an innovative way.

Addressing public problems in innovative ways, building profitable partnerships with private sectors, tapping into the rich knowledge base of communities and harnessing civic engagement for enhanced service delivery has never been the forte of Cameroon's public managers. And it is something they shall have to learn if the government hopes to deliver on the goals and objectives of its development programs.

---

11   Leadbeater, C., & Goss, S. (1998). *Civic Entrepreneurship.* London: Demos. p. 18.
12   Joan Vinyets is an innovation consultant, researcher and professor at the Universitat de Barcelona Business School.

Going back to the crises between the Kumbo Urban Council and the Kumbo Water Authority over the management of the Kumbo Water Scheme, a civic entrepreneur would have sought to leverage the comparative advantage and long experience of the KWA in the management of the Kumbo Water Scheme. In that sense, the KUC and the KWA could be encouraged to enter into a Memorandum of Understanding (MoU), whereby both parties would agree on certain performance standards and technical norms for delivering safe drinking water to people of Kumbo. Under the MoU, KWA could retain its operational role while the KUC could assume more oversight responsibilities. Both parties could create a joint technical inspection team charged with ensuring compliance with technical standards for the provision of safe drinking water. Where deficiencies are noted, parties shall work together to correct them. The focus and ultimate goal should be to deliver safe drinking water to the population of Kumbo Municipality in a sustained and cost effective manner. This is an outcome that surpasses all bureaucratic processes or political considerations. But unfortunately some Cameroon Public Managers do not always see things that way. They are bugged down by bureaucratic process and the need to enforce state privilege and state authority. I remember one government administrator telling me that by refusing to hand over the Kumbo Water Scheme to the KUC, the Fon of Nso and his people were "fighting the State', the implication here being that the Fon of Nso and his people are not part of the "State".

Civic entrepreneurship is about working with communities to address their everyday problems in an innovative and collaborative way. In their definition of civic entrepreneurship, Leadbeater and Goss stress the need to find new ways of combining resources and people, both public and private, to deliver better social outcomes. Another area I believe this combination of resources, both human and material, for better service delivery is in the security sector.

Civic Entrepreneurship Approach to Security Service Delivery

Sometime in December 2000, I went to the Central Police Station at Old Town Bamenda to see a relation of mine who was being detained there. I got to the front-desk (often referred to as the Charge Office) and politely asked an officer if he could tell me why the family member was detained and when he will be released or presented before the State Prosecutor. He said only the Commissioner in Charge of the Station could answer that. I demanded to know where I could find the Commissioner. The Officer said he didn't know the Commissioner's whereabouts nor did he know when he would be back in the office. At that point I asked if he could give me the Commissioner's cell phone number. The Officer looked me wide-eyed as if I had gone mad. *"How dare you ask for the Commissioner's number!"* he screamed. *"You think we give his number to just anybody?"*

The fun part is at that time I was also a serving Divisional Officer and so technically I was the Commissioner's boss. I wasn't "just anybody", as the Officer had imagined.

This incident, in a way, opened my eyes to how disconnected law enforcement officers can be from the public. In some countries police officers on the beat routinely give out their business cards to the population. But in Cameroon, a rank-and-file officer thought I should be insane to dare to ask for the mobile phone number of his Precinct Commander. The fact of the matter is, in spite of past efforts to bring law enforcement officers closer to the public (*police de proximité* as they call it in French) the relationship between the community and law enforcement officers (by which I mean Police and Gendarmes) has always been adversarial, confrontational and replete with mutual suspicion. Cameroon law enforcement officers treat their fellow citizens as if they are enemy combatants; as people not to be trusted. Law enforcement officers see the citizenry as a threat to them. As a result, the population has also developed some sort of a siege mentality vis-à-vis law enforcement officers. In fact, there is a saying in Cameroon that the fear of the Gendarme is the beginning of wisdom. This sums it all. Security and law enforcement officers are to be feared, not respected. As a consequence, the trust and the symbiotic relationship that should normally exist between the law enforcement community and the citizenry is markedly absent.

Any first time visitor travelling by road in Cameroon will be struck by the sheer number of security road blocks and check-points. They are everywhere. Twice in the last three decades or so, the President has ordered the dismantling of permanent security road blocks on the nation's highways. But the Police and Gendarmes simply ignored him. Between Bamenda and Bali, a distance of some 20 kms, there can be as much as four road blocks on any given day. The police and gendarmes manning them claim they are there to ensure security and enforce compliance with the Highway Code. Yet all commercial vehicles plying that road are always in violation of the Highway Code, as they are always over-loaded. It is not uncommon to see a driver sitting between two passengers while driving. The only reason law enforcement and security operations in Cameroon start and end on the highways is simply because it is lucrative venture. The security forces are there to collect and extort money from vehicular road users.

A civic entrepreneurial approach to security and law enforcement is therefore an imperative. Community policing best addresses this imperative.

Community Policing

"Community policing" sometimes known as "community-oriented polic-ing (COP)" is a strategy for preventing crime and ensuring the safety and security of citizens through building ties and working closely with members of the community.

The United States Department of Justice defines "community policing" as:
...a philosophy that promotes organizational strategies that support the systematic use of partnerships and problem-solving techniques to proactively address the imme-diate conditions that give rise to public safety issues such as crime, social disorder, and fear of crime.[13]

Whether it is viewed as a philosophy or as a strategy, the ultimate goal of community policing is to prevent crime and curb social disorder through functional partnerships between law enforcement agencies and the communi-ties they serve. In this regard, the US Department of Justice lays out three key components of community policing. These core components are:

* Community Partnerships - collaborative partnerships between the law enforcement agency and the individuals and organizations they serve to develop solutions to problems and increase trust in police.
* Organizational Transformation - the alignment of organizational management, structure, personnel, and information systems to support community partnerships and proactive problem solving.
* Problem Solving - the process of engaging in the proactive and sys-tematic examination of identified problems to develop and evaluate effective responses.

As a strategy, community policing puts the end user (that is communi-ties and individuals) at the center of policing. This is in marked contrast to what exists in Cameroon where security and law enforcement is a top-down, government-centric affair with very little community voice and participation. The strategy also emphasizes preventive action, building trust and the use of information systems and technology to fight crime and keep communities safe. Partnerships for enhanced safety and security within the nation's communities, towns and cities can be extended to include the private sector, the media, NGOs and community-based organizations.

Take a possible partnership between the private sector and law enforcement,

---

13   In "Community Policing Defined", a publication of the Community-Oriented Policing Services (COPS) of the U.S Department of Justice, 2012.

for instance.

If you visit any business district in any of Cameroon's towns or cities, you shall be sure to find armed law enforcement officers (police and gendarmes) standing guard at the doors, night and day. You see them in front of banks, super markets, insurance companies, hotels etc. These are hundreds of officers doing sentry duty. With a little bit of imagination and innovative spirit, and in partnership with law enforcement agencies, private businesses can be encouraged to take primary responsibility for their own security by recruiting trained security personnel, and installing round the clock video surveillance and monitoring equipment. In that case, rather than have law enforcement officers standing guard at their premises twenty-four-seven, the rapid intervention units of the police or the gendarmes can be called in when needed. In so doing, the hundreds, if not thousands, of law enforcement officers doing sentry duties in front of businesses shall be freed up and deployed to other more urgent tasks within the communities. Similarly, the nation's towns and cities could be carved out into "sectors" for community policing purposes. Each sector could then be assigned to a team of officers, whose responsibility it shall be to work with community leaders on a daily basis to assess the community's security challenges and develop community-based strategies on how to respond to them. In that regard, the hundreds of police officers manning roadblocks on the nation's highways for no other purpose than to extort money from road users, can be withdrawn and assigned to the sector community policing teams. The setting up of properly constituted Municipal Police Services proposed in the previous chapter, could fit well into this community policing scheme.

I am aware that to achieve this will require a complete paradigm and organizational culture shift within the Cameroonian law enforcement community. But I also do know that there are lots of civic entrepreneurs within that community willing and able to challenge the status quo. One of the key aspirations of Cameroon Vision 2035 is to build a *united and indivisible nation enjoying peace and security*. Building sustainable peace and security may continue to be elusive unless security and law enforcement managers in Cameroon adopt a civic entrepreneurial approach to preventing crime and ensuring the preservation of social order. I believe this can best be achieved through a bold and innovative community policing strategy, seamlessly wedded to the ongoing decentralization process in the country.

Strengthening Public Accountability

Until December 2019, Mr. Leubou Emmanuel was a mid-level civil servant little known to the Cameroon public. Nevertheless, as the head of the Computer Unit of the Department of Personnel Expenditures and Pensions in the Ministry of Finance, he wielded great influence over the salaries, pensions and other financial entitlements of civil servants. It is in that regard that he used his position to fraudulently manipulate the government payroll. It is reported that Leubou Emmanuel created fictitious salary accounts in the system,[14] and arranged for those salaries to be paid out to him every month, through a sophisticated network of accomplices at different levels of the Finance Ministry and the Central Treasury of Yaoundé. The fraudulent scheme is reported to have lasted for ten years. He was subsequently arrested, along with his accomplices, charged with the embezzlement of 5, 5 billion XAF (about USD 10 million), and sentenced to 104 years in prison.

This incident is not unusual in Cameroon. The fraudulent manipulation of the public payroll and the state budget by unscrupulous civil servants and vote holders for personal gain is a common phenomenon. How did a mid-level civil servant create and sustain a network for defrauding the State of billions of CFA for a decade?

This question points directly to Cameroon's weak and ineffectual public accountability framework; especially financial accountability.

Public Accountability and Democratic Governance

It was Benjamin Disraeli, a British Statesman, novelist and two-time Prime Minister between 1868, 1874–80, who famously wrote that *"all power is a trust; that we are accountable for its exercise; that from the people and for the people all springs, and all must exist"*.[15] The notion of public accountability is therefore closely tied to the practice of democratic governance and to the tenets of representative democracy. It emphasizes the need for trust between government and the governed and the efficient management of public resources. Public accountability demands responsiveness, responsibility and integrity on the part of public office holders. According to the North Ireland Open Government Network (NIOGN), public accountability "conveys the image of transparency

---

14   Some newspaper reports allege Emmanuel Leubou had created as much as 2,061 fake salary accounts that were yielding him some XAF 1.8 bn a month for a 10-year period.

15   Disraeli, B (1826), *Vivian Grey: A novel*, page 206. Cited on the website of the Controller and Auditor-General of New Zealand. https://oag.parliament.nz/2019/public-accountability/part2.htm

and trustworthiness and it holds strong promises of fair and equitable governance".[16] Singapore is known to have a strong public accountability framework with zero-tolerance for waste, inefficiency and corruption. The task of enforcing this rigorous public accountability framework falls to the Auditor-General. The Office of the Auditor-General of Singapore has a very simple, straightforward principle of public accountability:

> When a person is given the responsibility to hold, use or dispose of resources not belonging to him, he must be held fully answerable to the owner of the resources for what he does with them.[17]

This, in plain terms, is the very essence of public accountability and how it feeds into the principles and practice of democratic governance.

A strong public accountability system curbs waste and corruption, and ensures that resources intended for delivering services for the citizenry are used for that purpose. A weak public accountability does the exact opposite: encourages waste and corruption that go a long way to undermine public service provisioning.

Cameroon's Framework for Enforcing Public Accountability

Like most countries, Cameroon does have a public accountability framework derived from legislative, judiciary and executive (administrative) instruments and practices.

The Constitution of Cameroon establishes the principle of legislative oversight over the executive arm of government. Article 11, for instance, states that the executive arm of government shall be responsible to the National Assembly. In this regard, and as per Article 14(2) of the Constitution, parliament is empowered to control government action. Parliamentary oversight over the executive arm of government is consistent with Parliament's historical role as the "purse-holder" of the nation with primary responsibility to hold the executive arm of government accountable for the use of public funds appropriated to it by parliament. Since it is parliament that votes the National Budget, the responsibility to ensure transparent and efficient management of that budget devolves to it. This is the ultimate role of the legislature in matters of public accountability.

---

16   NIOGN Public Accountability Factsheet.

17   "*What is Public Accountability?*" a publication of the Office of the Auditor-General of Singapore, January 2018, p.2

In addition to legislative oversight, the judiciary also plays an important role in enforcing public accountability. Article 41 of the Constitution ascribes to the Audit Bench the power to control and adjudicate on public accounts as well as the accounts of public and semi-public enterprises. Other jurisdictions like the Special Crimes Tribunal and the High Courts play a more punitive role in the enforcement of public accountability measures.

There is an array of administrative outfits embedded within the government bureaucracy and public organizations charged with ensuring proper accountability for public funds and resources. There is the National Anti-Corruption Commission, which is supposedly autonomous but whose members are appointed by, and report to, the President. Each Ministry also has its own Anti-Corruption Unit. The National Anti-Corruption Commission and the ministerial Anti-Corruption Units are mandated to investigate and denounce acts of corruption that undermine public trust in government. The Ministry of State Control is a line ministry, embedded within the Presidency, entrusted with wide-ranging powers to control and investigate the proper of use of public resources in public and para-public institutions. It reports directly to the President, who alone decides what to do with the reports. The Directorate-General of the Budget in the Ministry of Finance also has its own team of Budget Controllers charged with investigating improper budgetary transactions and practices. Lastly, each ministerial department has a team of Inspector-Generals who are supposedly charged with the routine review of administrative processes and practices within their respective ministries to ensure that standards for public accountability and public service delivery are respected.

Conceptually, Cameroon seems to have a public accountability framework as one would expect to see in any progressive, democratic state. Unfortunately, like anything else in Cameroon, making the framework to function as it should is the biggest challenge. The ruling party's majority in both houses of parliament since the return to multiparty politics in 1990 makes it quasi-impossible for the legislature to exercise any meaningful control over the executive arm of government. Similarly, to have administrative departments embedded within, and reporting to, the executive branch of government trying to hold the same executive branch accountable is clearly an exercise in futility. Article 66 of the Constitution obligates all public office holders, especially vote holders and public accountants, to declare their assets upon assuming office and after leaving it. That article has never been implemented ever since it was written into the 1996 Constitution. To date only one politician is known to have ever declared his assets. That was Gustav Essaka, the late President and Founder of the "*Democratie*

Integrale du Cameroun" (DIC) political party.

I must however, aver that the Cameroon Government had in the early and mid-2000 taken some commendable measures aimed at strengthening transparency and public accountability, especially in the Public Finance Management (PFM) Sector. In a 2008 report, the World Bank lauded policy and institutional reforms the government had undertaken and which had led to some progress in budget reporting and transparency, public procurement and reduction of corruption. The Bank however, cautioned that Cameroon still had a long way to go to create an environment of strong governance and reduced corruption that is conducive to economic development. In that regard the Bank said it was willing to work with the Government on a project aimed at contributing towards the enhancement of transparency and efficiency in the Public Finance Management Sector and to strengthen accountability in the use of public resources, which would ideally lead to a more efficient service delivery.[18] This project was approved for implementation in 2008 and it is not hard to fathom how successful it was since in 2020, twelve years later, a mid-level civil servant was still able to swindle billions of francs CFA from the public payroll.

Proposed Public Accountability Framework for Enhanced Public Service Provisioning

Quite clearly the country's public accountability framework needs to be reviewed and strengthened. Within the purview of the refoundation of the Cameroon nation, I propose a framework that combines administrative and coercive organs of the state operating independently, autonomously but collaboratively, on the basis of powers conferred to them directly by the Constitution.

Curbing Corruption through Robust Judicial Action

I believe that curbing and fighting corruption is at the core of ensuring public (especially financial) accountability and enhancing service delivery. There is a simple formula for corruption:

Authority + Discretion - Accountability = Corruption

In other words, any authority that is exercised with total discretion and for which there is no accountability will inevitably lead to abuse and corruption. This to me seems to be exactly what is happening in Cameroon. There are Government Ministers and General Managers of State-Owned Enterprises who have been

---

18   World Bank Report No. AB1152: "Transparency and Accountability Capacity Development Project", June 2008.

in their posts for decades usually with nothing spectacular to show for it. They exercise a lot of discretionary powers over which they are hardly held accountable, until or unless they fall out of favor with the political establishment, then they are arrested, tried and jailed for corruption. Ministers and General Managers in Cameroon are known to manage their organizations' finances as if they were a petty cash or an imprest fund. They can do so with absolute impunity because the decision to hold them accountable before a court of law is largely political. It is the President and his Minister of Justice, not an independent judicial body, who decide who should be tried or not.

It is in this regard that I propose the setting up of independent and autonomous national prosecution body, to replace the current Legal Departments which are placed under the strict authority of the Minister of Justice. Such a body (of whatever name) shall be provided for in the Constitution and shall be funded directly by parliamentary appropriation. Its head may be nominated by the President of the Republic but confirmed by the Senate. He or she should serve for a fixed term and can only be removed from office through impeachment as provided for in the Constitution. An independent and autonomous national prosecution body, deriving its authority from the Constitution, free from executive interference and insulated from political pressure should be able to enforce public accountability in a fair, effective, timely and impartial manner.

The magnitude of corruption in Cameroon is so deep that an independent, autonomous national prosecution body, no matter how well-intentioned, shall not be do able to do it alone. The national prosecution body should therefore be part of a task-force that brings together other administrative bodies like the Budget Control Unit of the Ministry of Finance, the National Anti-Corruption Commission and the Ministry of State Control and the National Financial Investigation Agency. This will ensure that all investigations of financial and management improprieties end up with expedited judicial action.

Redesign of General Inspectorate Function

I propose a complete revamping of the General Inspectorate system. There is a common belief in Cameroon that the General Inspectorate of Ministries is a 'garage'. It is where the government assigns senior civil servants it doesn't know what to do with. Yet, Inspector Generals were supposed to be those overseeing administrative reforms and assisting the Ministers in ensuring public accountability within their ministries. The General Inspectorate should be taken away from Ministries and reconstituted as an independent administrative audit body, created under the constitution and funded directly from the State budget through parliamentary appropriation, and imbued with administrative, financial and operational autonomy. It could be renamed as Inspectorate General of Government, and it shall be charged with auditing government performance with regard to the implementation of public policy and compliance with administrative procedures. The Inspectorate General of Government can play a key role in the day-to-day evaluation of progress, or lack thereof, made by line Ministries towards the attainment of the goals and objectives of the national flagship development programs, to wit, Cameroon Vision 2035. In this way the Inspectorate General of Government shall be an external audit organization, not just holding government organizations accountable for performance but also providing strategic advice on how to improve their performance and streamline their processes such that they lead to better outcomes in public service delivery.

Competitive Processes for Hiring Senior Public Managers and Fixed Term Appointments

When public managers believe their positions are some sort of a sinecure granted to them as compensation for their political loyalty, the less they feel accountable. That is precisely the kind of attitude some public managers in Cameroon have adopted, especially those who have spent decades in the same position but whose longevity in those positions is not matched by their performance. That is why I propose the introduction of competitive processes in the hiring of public managers and fixed term appointments. The current practice of appointing managers for indeterminate periods has lent itself to abuse and the glorification of incompetence, both of which are deleterious to any form of public accountability. I understand that the authority to appoint to civil and military posts is a discretionary power accorded to the President of the Republic by the Constitution. Nonetheless, discretionary powers need not be exercised arbitrarily. Appointments to posts of responsibility in the civil service or in public organizations should be preceded by a competitive process aimed at selecting the most qualified candidate in a transparent and rational manner. In some critical instances appointments should be on a fixed-term, based on a performance contract or a well-defined, time-bound, scope of work.

Embracing E-Government

The Cameroon government needs to aggressively embrace e-government. The United Nations Public Administration Network has ascertained that the application of Information Communication and Technology (ICT) to the conduct of government business leads to greater efficiency and effectiveness in the delivery of public services to citizens and businesses. Through innovation and e-government, the U.N emphasizes:

> Governments around the world can be more efficient, provide better services, respond to the demands of citizens for transparency and accountability, be more inclusive and thus restore the trust of citizens in their governments.[19]

In Africa, countries like South Africa and Rwanda have adopted e-government with enduring benefits for public service delivery and accountability. This is an area that the Cameroon Government needs to embrace with fierce urgency. The digitalization or the transfer of some core government processes online shall go a long way to address the problem of administrative bottlenecks, inertia and the lack of celerity in public service delivery that the President has been decrying for nearly four decades now. Some baby steps have been taken with regard to e-government processes. For instance the University of Buea has for many years now introduced online applications which went a long way to eliminate the long lines that were known to form for days on end in front of the admission office. Similarly, the Department of Taxes has now made it possible to apply for and obtain tax payers' cards online. The General Delegation for National Security now has an online process for applying for passports. The Lands Department now uses geolocalisation tools to mark and identify landed property before it is transferred which has gone a long way to curb the dubious transfer of landed property. As commendable as these measures are, they are still inadequate. They need to be extended to more administrative processes, especially in the area of licensing. E-government shall help eliminate the long lines and over-crowding which have become common sights in front of government offices. NDS30 stresses the need for the "strategic management of the state". An aggressive e-government program can play a significant role in that regard.

Conclusion

Re-defining the role of the Central Government vis-à-vis the Regional and Local Councils, leveraging civic and social entrepreneurship, strengthening public accountability and building a viable e-government infrastructure can serve as strong building blocks for a new public service delivery model for the country; a model capable of driving economic growth and rapid social transformation.

---

19   www.publicadministration.un.org

However, to achieve this will require a strong, visionary leadership. Chinua Achebe once wrote that the problem with Africa is simply and squarely a failure of leadership. In Chapter One, I talked about how this country is being dexterously held back by a leadership that has run out of ideas on how to move the country forward. The rebirth of this country, through the renewal of the dream of its founders, demands that we correct its leadership quandary. In the next chapter, therefore, I shall expound on what I believe the new leadership prototype for the rebirth of this nation should look like.

Chapter Five

Envisioning a New Political Leadership Paradigm

Dubai is among the best known cities in the world. The city is so famous that many people think it is a country of its own. But the truth is Dubai is just one, albeit the most famous, of seven emirates that make up the federation of the United Arab Emirates. Not too long ago Dubai was nothing but a small desert town, much like Ngaoundere or Kumba or Garoua. Today it is an ultramodern, high-tech city and a favorite tourist's destination.

None of this would have been possible without the strong vision and near revolutionary, transformational, leadership of Dubai's rulers. Since coming to power in 2006, the current ruler of Dubai, Sheik Mohammed bin Rashid Al Maktoum, has relentlessly pursued the city's transformational agenda begun in 1958 by his father, Sheik Rashid Bin Saeed Al Maktoum. Sheik Mohammad is largely credited with the modern day transformation of Dubai from a dusty desert outpost to a futuristic global city.

The Example of the Leader of Dubai

During a 2007 interview with the American television chain, CBS News, journalist Steve Kroft asked Sheik Mohammad:

"What are you trying to do here? What do you want this place to be?"

The Sheik's answer was sleek, simple and direct

"I *want it to be number one, not in the region but in the world"*, he replied without batting an eyelid.

"Number one in everything – higher education, health, housing, just giving my people the highest way of living", he added.

And when Steve Kroft sought to know why the haste? Why the sense of urgency? Why try to do in five years what most people will do in a lifetime? Sheik Mohammad bin Rashid Al Maktoum's response was again simple and direct.

"I want my people to live the good healthcare now, to be in the highest school now.

Not in twenty years", he retorted.

In a 2012 publication, Sheik Mohammad wrote at length about his vision and the kind of leadership he believes is needed for the economic and social transformation of not just Dubai, but of the UAE and the Arab world at large. As far as the Sheik was concerned the crisis and disunity that plague the Arab world is one of leadership, management and egotism. This is the kind of crisis which is bound to happen when:

> ...lust for power prevails over granting people the love and care they deserve and the destiny of one individual become more important than that of a whole nation. This is also what happens when the interest of some groups and cliques benefitting from certain leaders are served instead of those of the people.[1]

The Sheik showcases what he calls the UAE and Dubai's "distinctive development experience" as a good example of what can be accomplished when *"God blesses a country with unselfish leadership that strives for the good of its people and not its own"*. Good leadership, Sheik Mohammad avers, puts the interests of the community as a whole before those of any specific group.[2] The ruler of Dubai says his goal is to make of the Emirate *"...an international pioneering hub of excellence and creativity...and the world's premier trade, tourism and services destination in the twenty-first century"*. And he hopes to accomplish this goal through dedicated leadership, building state of the art infrastructure, showing his people the right direction and nurturing their potential for innovation, creativity and self-confidence. Dubai, the Sheik avows, "will never settle for anything less than first place."

The results have simply been mind-boggling.

In 1990 there was only one skyscraper in the city. Today, there are an estimated 148,917 high rise buildings, including the Burj Khalifa, said to be the tallest building in the world. Dubai has been dubbed the world's largest construction site. The city is a recognized global finance hub and the fourth most visited city in the world as of 2018. In 2016 it hosted 14.9 million overnight visitors and was expected to reach 20 million by 2020.[3] Cameroon's population

---

1   Al Maktoum, M. b. R. (2012). *My vision: challenges in the race for excellence*. Dubai: Motivate Publishing. p.5
2   Ibid, p.6.
3   This is according to a 2017 Gulf News report.

is almost eight times that of Dubai (3.3 million as against 26 million) yet in 2018, Dubai's GDP was almost three times that of Cameroon (USD 108 bn as against USD 38.7 bn). That is what bold, audacious, visionary, people-centered leadership can achieve.

But to bring the example closer to home, I shall consider the example of the African nation of Botswana.

The Example of Botswana

The Southern African nation of Botswana, with a population of 2.3 million, is often described as the continent's oldest democracy. When Botswana gained independence in 1966 it was one of the poorest countries on earth. The country was said to have just 12 km of paved roads, 22 university graduates and 100 secondary school graduates.[4] In just three decades after independence the country was able to transform into an upper middle-income economy with a stable and consistent economic growth.[5] In the 1960s, Botswana's GDP per capita (i.e., the purchasing power parity) was estimated at 70 USD. In 2015, the GDP per capita had risen to 18,825 USD. The country has one of the highest GDP per capita and the fourth largest gross national income in Africa. Its standard of living and its human development index are also among the highest in Sub Sahara Africa.[6] Botswana is considered as a very stable democracy based on the rule of law and with a very low incidence of corruption. In fact Transparency International routinely ranks it among the least corrupt countries in Africa.

This transformation could not have been possible without the visionary, transformational leadership qualities of Botswana's political leaders, especially its founding President, Sir Seretse Khama and his immediate successors. The link between good leadership and the political and economic transformation of Botswana has been strikingly summed up by authors, Sebudubudu and Both-omilwe, in these words:

> Botswana has been able to transform itself from a position of desola-
> tion at independence to one of an upper middle income country by the
> 1990s. It is today held as an economic and political success story that can
> offer lessons to other African countries. This is remarkable by African

4   Acemoglu, Johnson and Robinson "An African Success Story: Botswana" in https://economics.mit.edu/files/284

5   See Maundeni, Z., Mpabanga, D., & Mfundisi, A. (2007). *Consolidating Democratic Governance in Southern Africa: Botswana.*

6   According to CIA's "The World Factbook" of 2014

standards. Botswana's transformation was possible in part because of the good leadership and good policy decisions. The case of Botswana shows that leadership is a crucial success factor for any country's development prospects."[7]

And yes it truly is. Immediately after gaining independence, President Khama launched a robust economic program aimed at transforming the country into an export-based economy. From the outset he embraced free market economy principles. He instituted strong anti-corruption measures, increased personal freedoms and consciously promoted liberal democracy and the rule of law. The country's lean civil service was transformed into a corruption-free, merit-based public workforce. Public revenues earned from exports were invested in infrastructure, healthcare and education, thereby guaranteeing a high standard of living for the population and sustained economic growth for at least three decades. Botswana's political and economic transformation has largely been attributed to a combination of transformational political leadership and strong, inclusive institutions.

Basic Concepts of Leadership

I have used the examples of Dubai and Botswana because I believe they serve as examples of the kind of leadership paradigm needed for the refoundation of the Cameroon nation: audacious and transformational.

The last fifty years have seen an increase in scholastic research on the subject of leadership, especially, political leadership. In the process, new and innovative theories, doctrines and frameworks for defining who a true leader is or what leadership entails, have emerged. While it has never been easy to agree on a specific definition of the concept of "leadership" social scientists and scholars seem to have a consensus on its core components in the twenty-first century.

The Northouse Theory of Leadership

Peter Northouse, a leading researcher in leadership theory and practice, defines leadership as *"a process whereby an individual influences a group of individuals to achieve a common goal"*.[8] Northouse's definition of leadership is couched in four over-arching components which he considers central to both the concept

7   Sebudubudu, D., & Botlhomilwe, M. Z. (2012). The critical role of leadership in Botswana's development: What lessons? *Leadership, 8*(1), 29-45.

8   Northouse, P. G. (2013). *Leadership Theory and Practice.* Los Angeles: SAGE Publications p. 5

and the phenomenon of leadership.

First, leadership is a process. This in effect, means that is not a trait or a characteristic that resides in the leader. Rather, it is a transaction that occurs between the leader and followers. In that sense leadership can be viewed as an interactive event available to everyone and not just to a formally designated leader in the group.

Second, leadership is about how a leader affects followers. A leader must be able to influence his/her followers and without influence, Northouse says, leadership cannot be deemed to exist.

Third, Northouse understands leadership as a group activity, for it is within a group context that leadership emerges. The group could be a community, an association, an organization, a political or social movement. In that light, the ultimate aim of leadership is to influence a group of individuals towards a common cause.

Lastly, leadership is about achieving common goals. A leader must necessarily direct his or her energies towards individuals who are trying to achieve something together. This implies that both the leader and the follower must have a certain commonality of purpose. And it is this commonality of purpose, Northouse stresses, that ascribes to leadership an ethical dimension. The absence of mutual purpose between a leader and followers implies a leadership that is forced or coerced and therefore unethical.[9]

Drawing from Northouse's definition and his four components of leadership, it is easy to see what leadership is not. Leadership is not a character or behavioral trait. It is not a functional title or a job description. It is definitely not the position or some sort of authority that an individual holds within a community, an organization or an association. Leadership, simply put, is the ability to influence a group of individuals towards achieving a common, mutual purpose.

Transformational Versus Transactional Leadership

At the beginning of this chapter, I lauded Sheik Maktoum and Sir Seretse Khama's transformational leadership qualities and posited them as the kind of leadership paradigm central to the refoundation agenda of the Cameroon nation. But what exactly is transformational leadership? The concept has been around for some time but was popularized by political historian and sociologist, James McGregor Burns, in the later part of the 1970s.

9   Ibid, p. 6.

The J.M. Burns Concept of Transformational Leadership

In his 1978 treatise on the subject, Burns defined transformational leadership as the process whereby *"leaders and followers raise one another to higher levels of motivation and morality".*[10] For Burns, a leader can be considered as "transformational" if and only if he or she is committed to the collective good. In that regard, Burns was keen to differentiate between a leader and a power-holder. He argued that while leadership is an aspect of power, the two differ in the sense that power-holders pursue their personal goals while leaders are concerned with satisfying both the needs of followers as well as their own. Where leadership is not transformational, Burns further asserted, it may be transactional i.e., a simple exchange of valued gifts between leader and follower with no enduring purpose. According to Tracey and Hinkin, Transactional leadership is based on *"bureaucratic authority and legitimacy within the organization".* As a Consequence, transactional leaders *"emphasize work standards, assignments, and task-oriented goals…"* and *"…tend to focus on task completion and employee compliance".* In addition, such leaders *"…rely quite heavily on organizational rewards and punishments"* to influence employee performance. [11]

The Four Dimensional Construct of Transformational Leadership

Over the years, scholarly research on the subject of transformational leadership has deepened. Bass and Avolio have developed a four-dimensional construct of transformational leadership commonly referred to as the four I's. These are:

1. Idealized influence, or charisma: Transformational leaders have an uncanny ability to make you want to follow the vision they establish.
2. Inspirational motivation: Communication is a vehicle of inspiration for transformational leaders; they use words to encourage others and inspire action.
3. Intellectual stimulation: Transformational leaders stretch others to think more deeply, challenge assumptions, and innovate.
4. Individualized concern: Finally, while focused on the common good, transformational leaders show care and concern for individuals.[12]

---

10   Burns, J. M. (1978). *Leadership.* New York: Harper & Row. p.20

11   Tracey, J. B., & Hinkin, T. R. (1998). Transformational Leadership or Effective Managerial Practices? *Group & Organization Management, 23*(3), 220-236. p.5

12   Bass, B. M., & Avolio, B. J. (Eds.). (1994). *Improving organizational effectiveness through transformational leadership.* Thousand Oaks, CA, US: Sage Publications, Inc.

Relevance of Leadership Concepts to the Cameroon Context

The question that may be asked at this point is of what relevance are these leadership theories to the Cameroonian context and how do they fit into this treatise? I have taken the pains to lay out these different theories and frameworks of leadership because they shall form the basis of my assessment of leadership practices in Cameroon since unification. They shall also show how our current leadership quandary is making it impossible for this nation to rise up to the promise and vision of its founders.

The history of this country is replete with examples of individuals, most of them with no official titles, who led and inspired multitudes towards the achievement of a common, mutual purpose. In our never-ending endeavor to rise above the challenges of providing quality education to our children, or of improving our diet and wellbeing through agriculture or of enhancing livelihoods through community savings and self-help schemes, or of improving the health of the population, leaders have emerged and have risen to the occasion. In Chapter Three I cited examples of individuals and groups who took laudable initiatives and innovations that led to the creation of reputable institutions like the PNEU, the GCE Board, and the Cooperative Credit Unions. These were also expressions of transformational leadership. I shall briefly revisit some of them, but this time with the objective of highlighting and showcasing how, under their leadership, near revolutionary changes were made in some critical areas of our national life.

Examples of Contemporary Transformational Leadership

The Creation of PNEU and the GCE Board

It was under the leadership of Hon. Gwen Burnley and others that the Parents National Education Union (PNEU), grew out of a home-schooling arrangement in a garage to become one of the best and the most prestigious network of institutions of elementary education in this country. In 1993, Mr. Azong Wara and his colleagues of the Teachers Association of Cameroon (TAC), in a concrete display of transformational leadership, inspired and led a broad-based movement of teachers, parents and students to demand reforms in the organization of official end-of-course examinations. The teachers and parents were irked by what was clearly an attempt to undermine the credibility of end-of-course certificate examinations of the Anglophone Sub-system of education, notably the General Certificate of Examination (GCE), thereby comprising the future of Anglophone students. The result was the creation of the GCE Board.

The Origins of the Credit Union Movement

In 1963, Rev Father Anthony Jansen, a Dutch Mill Hill Missionary, started a small savings scheme for his parishioners in the North-Western town of Njinikom, with 16 members and a total savings of CFA 2100.[13] On 15 May 1965, the scheme was formally registered as the Njinikom Cooperative Credit Union. This was the beginning of a movement which would grow and blossom under the leadership of a young Catholic School teacher, M.T. Banseka. Mr. Banseka is credited with the popularization of the credit union movement in the Bamenda Grassfields, especially in his role as the pioneer manager of the Cameroon Credit Union League, the umbrella organization that oversees the credit union movement. The movement has grown exponentially with enormous benefits to its members. There is hardly any village in Anglophone Cameroon without a cooperative credit union scheme. The credit union is Cameroon's pioneer and most enduring micro-finance scheme. David Grace, Senior Vice President of Association Services at the World Council of Credit Unions (WOCCU) once described the credit union system in Cameroon as *"one of the greatest success stories in WOCCU's 40 years"*.[14] None of these achievements could have been possible without the stellar and inspiring leadership qualities of the pioneers of the movement – men like M.T. Banseka.

Pa S.Y. Tondo and the Advent of Fish Farming

Sometime in the mid-1950s, a young Basel Mission School Head teacher, Samuel Yasom Tondo, made a small entry into his personal diary, *"What can I do to improve on the diet of my people?"* Somehow, he decided that he could do this by introducing fish protein into the people's daily eating habits. But for this to happen, the people needed to first of all have access to fish. And how were they going to have access to fish in a highland area with no sea and no fish-seeded lakes and rivers? The answer lay in the development of inland, fresh water fishing.

For the three decades that followed that diary entry, Pa Tondo (as he came to be fondly called) developed a near obsession with inland fishery. He ingeniously constructed ponds and diverted stream-water into them to fill them up. He later caught fish in nearby streams, put them in his ponds and fed them with rudimentary fish-feed to enable them multiply. His objective was to gradually introduce badly needed fish protein into the diet of a community whose staple diet was carbohydrates from cocoyams and other tubers. The British Colonial

---

13 In 2013 the Njinikom Cooperative Credit Union reported a membership of 3,612 and total shares/savings of more than CFA 160 Million
14 WOCCU Press Release "Cameroon CUs Overcoming Challenges, Growing Membership".

Administration of the time was very impressed with his ingenuity and dedication to fish farming and sent him to Nigeria to study fresh-water fish farming. Upon his return he was absorbed into the West Cameroon Civil Service as Technical Officer in charge of Fish Farming. In that capacity, he toured all of West Cameroon, to campaign for, and to encourage communities and individuals alike to take up fish farming. After reunification in 1972. Mr. Tondo was deployed to the national Ministry of Agriculture in Yaoundé as Service Head in charge of Fish Farming. One of his greatest achievements during his tenure was the creation of fish farming demonstration centers in Yaoundé itself, relics of which can still be seen today below the student residential area of the University of Yaoundé, commonly known as Bonamoussadi. He also championed the setting up of a modern Fish Farming Station in Ku-Bome, Mbengwi, with technical assistance and funding from USAID. After retiring from the civil service in 1980, Pa Tondo still pursued his passion for fish farming. He created his own personal fish farm and used it to teach interested groups and individuals alike, basic fish farming techniques as well as the benefits of consuming freshwater fish.

At his death in 1996, his personal fish farm had a total of twelve ponds. I had the privilege of meeting Pa Samuel Yasom Tondo during my time as First Assistant Senior Divisional Officer for Momo Division. I also felt highly honored when his family asked me to be the keynote speaker at his funeral. At that funeral, speaker after speaker (including the Hon. S.T. Muna[15]) lauded Pa Tondo's profound leadership attributes and the genuine concern he had for the welfare of his people. He is almost singlehandedly responsible for promoting fish-farming in post-independence Cameroon, and for influencing changes in the diet of his cherished Meta Clan, through the introduction of fish into their daily eating habits. To this day, the people of Meta directly associate fish with Pa Tondo. In fact his people fondly nicknamed him *The Fish Administrator*. Through relentless advocacy and leadership, Pa Tondo was able to convince, first the West Cameroon State Government and later the National Government, to adopt the development of inland fisheries as a means of providing a protein dietary supplement and additional income for Cameroon's rural populations. And all this began as a simple diary entry.

Roland Fomundam and Innovations in Greenhouse Farming

In Cameroon, and indeed in most of Africa, farming is viewed as a profession

---

15   Former Prime Minister of West Cameroon, former Vice President of the Federal Republic of Cameroon and Former Speaker of the Cameroon National Assembly.

or an activity reserved for the rural peasantry. The image of a farmer is often that of a poor peasant dressed in ragged, dirty clothes and carrying rudimentary farm tools. But there is a young Cameroonian who has made it his life's mission to change all of that. His name is Roland Fomundam.

Roland describes himself as a "...*serial social entrepreneur with an aspiration for greatness*".[16] And it is not difficult to fathom why. In 2015, Roland Fomundam created Greenhouse Ventures, which he describes as a social enterprise dedicated to *"developing and deploying affordable greenhouse technology in Cameroon and many parts of Africa"*. As a company, Greenhouse Ventures promotes sustainable agriculture and hopes to become a pacesetter in the development of greenhouse technology and for the production of garden crops such a tomatoes, peppers, strawberries, spinach and flowers. Mr. Fomundam says his focus is on developing essential technologies with the ultimate aim of becoming *"a house of innovations for several farm technologies"*.[17]

Through Greenhouse Ventures, Roland Fomundam has changed both the notion and the perception of farming in Cameroon. Urban youths are becoming increasingly interested in agriculture. Farming is no longer seen as a profession for the rural poor or a hobby for the urban elite, but as a gainful enterprise that can be pursued in both urban and rural environments. Apart from its economic benefits, Roland's greenhouse technology innovations have the potential to revolutionize land use in Cameroon. The ability to grow more crops all year round on smaller parcels of land can go a long way to reduce the deadly land disputes that have become so common in Cameroon. Like Pa Samuel Yasom Tondo before him, Roland is also interested in inland fishery and has integrated fish farming into his greenhouse farms. His passion is working with the youth, to arouse their interest in agriculture as a gainful venture. In that regard he has opened the first ever greenhouse technology training center in Cameroon. Mr. Fomundam's vision and expectations are pretty simple, straightforward but poignant:

> Someday, these greenhouse farms will represent the nation - they will become an emblem for growth and innovation. Someday, Cameroonian youths will make a living from these farms - many of them will become millionaires. [18]

---

16   See his Facebook Profile at https://www.facebook.com/fomundam
17   Culled from the company's website www.greenhouseventures.cm
18   From a post on Roland Fomundam's Facebook page of 20th January 2020.

The reason I chose these five case studies is three-fold.

First, they best encapsulate Peter Northouse's notion of leadership as a process whereby an individual influences a group of individuals to achieve a common goal. Second, they vividly capture the essentials of Bass and Avolio's four I's of transformational leadership, to wit: idealized charisma based on a sound vision, inspiring others to act and take up new challenges, high sense of innovation and concern for the welfare of individuals. The development of inland fishing, the establishment of PNEU schools, the creation of cooperative credit union schemes and the setting up of the GCE Board were bold and innovative projects that many considered too advanced, and maybe too sophisticated for that time. They needed an equally bold and innovative leadership for them to succeed. Today a young man is following in the footsteps of his forebears to contrive a revolution in farming through a bold and innovative greenhouse farming experiment. He is on course to become the greatest transformational leader of his generation. And third, these examples show a profound commitment on the part of these leaders to achieve a common good and to ensure the welfare and the wellbeing of society, which is the hallmark of transformational leadership. It is also important to note that at the time these leaders commenced their quest to change the world around them, none of them, except Hon Gwen Burnley, held any formal, significant position of authority or political power. They were driven by a burning desire to make life better for their community through change and innovation.

This brings me to the issue of the exercise of political leadership in Cameroon. But before I get to that I shall first of all revisit some concepts and theoretical considerations of political leadership.

Notions of Political Leadership and their Contextual Relevance to Cameroon

Academic scholarship on the subject of political leadership tends to describe its nature, its content and its core characteristics but without offering a clear-cut definition of what it is. Joseph Masciulli et al., for instance, contend that the concept of political leadership is difficult to define "*essentially, because it is dependent on institutional, cultural and historical contexts and situations…*" However, they offer some "elements" that should be considered in any definition of political leadership. These include, the personality and traits of a leader or leaders, including her or his ethical and cultural character; the traits and ethical-cultural character of the followers with whom the leader interacts; the societal or organizational context in which the leader–follower interaction occurs – general culture, political culture, political climate, norms, and institutions; the agenda of collective problems or tasks which confront the leaders and followers in particular historical situations; the nature of the leader's interpretive judgment, since situations do not define themselves, but have to be defined by leaders' insights accepted by the followers; the means – material and intangible – that the leaders use to attain their ends and/or their followers' goals; the effects or results of leadership (whether real or symbolic, long lasting or transient).[19]

Leadership, the authors argue, is at the core of government and governance because:

> ....weak leadership contributes to government failures, and strong leadership is indispensable if the government is to succeed. Wise leadership secures prosperity in the long run; foolhardy leadership may bring about a catastrophe. The lack of leadership routinizes governance. Its political and creative aspects fade away: it becomes no different from administration, focusing solely on pattern maintenance and repetition of the same.[20]

Building on their constitutive elements of political leadership and the way they relate to the exercise of governmental power, Masciulli et al. define political leadership "*... as a rather unique set of power relations and influences that is exercised over a broad range of nationally and globally salient issue areas and from a position of authoritative preponderance involving ideologies and ethic*".[21]

The Exercise of Political Leadership in Cameroon

Since independence, Cameroon has had just two presidents. Its first President, Ahmadou Ahidjo ruled the country for twenty-two years (from January 1960 to November 1982) before handing over to the current President who has been in power since the 6th of November 1982.

Ahidjo was by all accounts an autocrat who ruled the country with an iron fist. And I use the word 'rule' here (instead of "govern") very deliberately. He was intolerant of dissent and saw no merit in consultative or consensual politics. However, those who were close to him say he did have a deep sense of patriotism and an unparalleled love for Cameroon. He was imbued with a

---

19   Masciulli, J., Molchanov, M. A., & Knight, W. A. (2009). Political Leadership in Context. In J. Masciulli, M. A. Molchanov, & W. A. Knight (Eds.), *The Ashgate Research Companion to Political Leadership*. London & New York: Routledge. p. 5-6

20   Ibid, p. 3.

21   Ibid p.6.

vision and a mission: that of making Cameroon a great, prosperous and united nation. Ahidjo's leadership qualities were more transactional. Given his autocratic and highhanded tendencies, he was more feared than respected. And so whatever influence he had over the Cameroon polity was more or less coerced. His leadership hinged on his bureaucratic authority and legitimacy, to quote Tracey and Hinkin. He wielded absolute power which allowed him to influence others from a position of authoritative preponderance. And from that position he was able to leverage group influence by dishing out punishment and rewards.

I want to believe that as a political leader, President Amadou Ahidjo was genuinely concerned with the common good. But I harbor strong doubts that he was able to raise both himself and his people to a higher level of motivation and morality. The institutionalization of the one party state and the abolition of the federation are important watersheds in the history of this country. But they were somewhat coerced and were devoid of the commonality of purpose that should inform such decisions. I would even go as far as to say the creation of the single party and the abolition of the federal state structure were primarily intended to consolidate Ahidjo's personal power and sense of grandeur. President Ahidjo did possess some flashes of charisma and was a good communicator. But he can be said to have lacked the intellectual stimulation and the individualized concern that are some of the hallmarks of transformational leadership. Given his highhandedness, and considering his obsession with the magnificence of power, it can be said that he deeply cared about Cameroon the country, but probably not about Cameroonians. Ahidjo's transactional, top-down leadership model has endured to this day.

His successor, Mr. Paul Biya, came to power promising a different leadership model; one that was transformational. While it can be said that he lacked the charisma and communication skills of his predecessor, he however, was imbued with a certain level of intellectual stimulation that underpinned his vision. Unlike Ahidjo who had just secondary school education, Mr. Biya was a university graduate with advanced degrees obtained in France. He came to power in 1982 promising a New Deal Era in which state affairs shall be managed with rigor and moralization. Five years later, in 1987, he published his seminal work "Communal Liberalism" in which he laid out his political philosophy and his vision for the country. He was asserting his academic and intellectual credentials as a transformational leader. J.M. Burns believed that transformational leadership comes from intellectuals because the leadership of intellectuals *begins in a potent vision of what is and what might be, and grows in their ability to convey that vision to the people in need of it*. Professor of Global Affairs and Associate Fellow at Chatham House, Katherine Morton takes a broader view of the subject by establishing a nexus between leadership by intellectuals and institutional and policy innovation. In that regard she holds that:

> ...intellectual leadership relies upon the power of ideas to shape the thinking behind the principles underpinning institutional arrangements, guide understanding of the issues at stake, and orient policy towards alternative options.[22]

However, Burns cautions that would-be followers will respond to the transformational leader only *"if the new frame articulated by creative leadership speaks directly to them, to their underlying wants, discontents, and hopes"*.[23] Mr. Biya's New Deal vision and his political philosophy of Communal Liberalism instantly struck a chord with the vast majority of Cameroonians who were yearning for change after twenty- two years of Ahidjo's autocratic rule. But as it turned out, that was not to be.

Less than a year after taking over office in November 1982, the relationship between Mr. Biya and the person he was fond of referring to as his "illustrious predecessor", former President Ahidjo, soured considerably. Soldiers loyal to the former President staged a failed coup to overthrow Mr. Biya on 4 April 1984, barely a year and the half after he took office. He was clearly shaken by the failed coup attempt and so he sought to rid himself from Ahidjo's influence. By 1985, with the creation of the Cameroon People's Democratic Movement (CPDM) Mr. Biya can be said to have successfully won his battle against Ahidjo and cemented his authority on the country. It is important to highlight that before the creation of the CPDM, Mr. Biya had already started making some bold political reforms mainly aimed at injecting some veneer of competition in the selection of candidates for elections, albeit, within the lone-party framework of the Cameroon National Union (CNU), the political organization he inherited from Ahidjo. A 1983 modification of the constitution made it possible for multiple candidates to vie for the presidency. All the candidate needed to do was to obtain 500 signatures (50 from each of the ten provinces) from prominent

---

22   Morton, K. (2017). Political Leadership and Global Governance: Structural Power Versus Custodial Leadership. *Chinese Political Science Review, 2*(4), 477-493. doi:10.1007/s41111-017-0089-4 p. 482

23   Cited in Reid, W. M., & Dold, C. J. (2018). Burns, Senge, and the Study of Leadership. *Open Journal of Leadership, 7*(1), 89-116. p.94

personalities such as locally elected officials, traditional chiefs, Members of Parliament, Field Administrative Officers and Members of the Central Committee of the Cameroon National Union. Of course, this was never going to happen as none of these officials, who owed their positions to the President, was ever going to nominate someone else to run against him. In 1988, during the parliamentary elections, Mr. Biya, as Head of State and Chairperson of the ruling CPDM party, allowed for competitive process within his party, whereby two party lists (Green and Khaki) were submitted to the electorate from which to choose. This opening of the political space, even within the one-party system, was very much acclaimed by the population and somewhat acted as the precursor to the return to multipartyism a few years later.

The return to multiparty politics came with a different set of challenges for Mr. Biya. The nascent opposition parties, pressure groups and movements that emerged after 1990 posed a serious threat to Mr. Biya's power. Soon he found himself fighting, literally, for his political survival. As he sought to deal with this new threat and re-consolidate his hold on the country, he also began adopting Ahidjo's authoritarian, top-down, transactional leadership model. And that is the political leadership model that prevails to this day.

Political Leaders as Power Holders

Within the context of Cameroon politics, the word "leadership" can be considered a misnomer. What obtains in Cameroon is more of "rulership". The political elite of this country (by which I mean government ministers, members of national assembly, mayors, and all those wielding some form of governmental authority, or play a public management role at any level) are more of power-holders and rulers, not leaders in the sense that Burns and Northouse envisaged it. And they are hardly ever willing or able to go beyond the influence they wield as power-holders to become true leaders. In a representative democracy like the one we are striving for, citizens elect politicians or support their nominations to positions of authority so that they can speak for and represent the citizens. In a true expression of political agency, political leaders are expected to exemplify and articulate the beliefs, wishes, desires, positions and aspirations of the population. They must act as citizens' representatives at all levels of the state. Unfortunately this is hardly ever the case. As soon as politicians are elected, or individuals are appointed to positions of power and responsibility, their loyalty is immediately directed upwards, towards the higher echelons of power, not downwards towards those who are supposedly their constituents or followers. A good example is what happens in the National Assembly. At the start of each legislative year, the Members of Parliament must elect a Speaker. And quite often, the elected Speaker in his opening speech would invariably start by thanking the Head of State for his election, not his peers who elected him.

In recent times this reversal of the leadership-followership loyalties and the obfuscation of the notions of political agency were very evident in 2016, during the outbreak of the current crisis raging in Anglophone Cameroon.

Political Leadership and the Management of the Anglophone Crisis

In 2016 Anglophone teachers and lawyers took to the streets to demand an end to the marginalization of the Anglophone minority through thinly veiled attempts by the Central Government to destroy their educational and judicial systems. Even though it was evident that the lawyers and the teachers had considerable support from a vast majority of the population, the Anglophone political elite (especially those affiliated to the ruling CPDM party) refused to support their cause. Like true power-holders, they were looking out for their own interest and pursuing their personal goals; they were not looking out for the interest, or articulating the wishes and desires of the population. Some of them took turns on national radio and television shows to argue that there was no marginalization of Anglophones in Cameroon; that the agitating teachers and lawyers were a bunch of troublemakers with no mandate to speak for Anglophone Cameroon.

At some point someone came up with the brilliant idea that the best way to address the crisis that was playing out in the streets of Anglophone Cameroon was to organize CPDM marches in Buea and in Bamenda to show support for the Head of State and National Chairperson of the CPDM. The first march in Buea took place without incident. But when, on 8 December 2016, CPDM stalwarts tried to organize a similar one in Bamenda it did not go exactly as planned. Enraged youths, determined to stop the march, took to the streets. Violent confrontations between the youths and the security forces ensued. Lives were lost. Public property, including a local police precinct was burnt. The marchers, among whom was the Prime Minister and many of his cabinet ministers, had to be expeditiously scuttled out of town for their own safety.

Rebuke of the Anglophone Political Leadership

What the youths of Bamenda did that day was a resounding rebuke of the political leadership, or what passes for it, in Anglophone Cameroon. Their so-called leaders had clearly chosen their sides and it was not with them. At a time when the people needed them most, the leadership was found wanting.

And in the months and years that would follow, the people would turn towards a different set of "leaders" with devastating consequences. The savage, armed conflict that is today raging in Anglophone Cameroon may have been averted if the political elite for once showed mettle and courage and spoke truth to power. The situation in the streets of Anglophone Cameroon at the time demanded sterling leadership. But this was never forthcoming. I must however, note the efforts made by the opposition Social Democratic Front (SDF) members of parliament, notably Hon. Joseph Wirba, to force a parliamentary debate on the conflict in Anglophone Cameroon. Similarly, CPDM Senator, Nfon Victor Mukete tried to elicit some action from his colleagues from the floor of the Senate. But even these token efforts were thwarted by the CPDM majority which continued to spout out the official government line that there was no Anglophone Problem worth debating.

Institutional Leadership in Conflict Management

Quite often it is during a period of crisis and conflict that the mutually reinforcing role of political leadership and political institutions find an enhanced relevance. Katherine Morton has noted, and rightly so, that "...*the history of institution building suggests that political leadership matters most at times of crisis; and that crises often act as catalysts for institutional innovation*".[24] As I mentioned in Chapter Two, Cameroon's political institutions are very extractive in nature, tailored to the needs, and made to promote and defend the interests of a ruling elite. They serve to perpetuate a political hegemony. So predictably, these institutions, especially parliament and the executive branch of government, are usually slow to self-innovate as a means of addressing crisis and conflicts. Institutional approaches to conflict management demand that conflicts should be managed within the institutions of state, not through adhoc mechanisms. But when faced with severe crises and conflicts that can make or blemish the State, Cameroon's political leadership class has often resorted to adhoc methods, or to deny and deflect tactics.

I shall go back to its management of the current Anglophone crisis, with particular emphasis on role of the National Assembly, to explain this point.

A National Assembly, by definition and by character, is the one institution of governance where the great issues affecting the nation, or likely to impact its destiny, are tabled and debated with a view to finding sustainable solutions. It

---

24   Morton, K. (2017). Political Leadership and Global Governance: Structural Power Versus Custodial Leadership. *Chinese Political Science Review*, *2*(4), 477-493.

is often from the floor of a national parliament that strong political leadership springs forth and great debates enriched by opposing viewpoints help shape the destiny of a nation. By mid-2017, it was becoming increasingly clear that the conflict in Anglophone Cameroon was turning violent with deleterious consequences to the security and territorial integrity of the nation. A half-hearted attempt by the Prime Minister to engage in dialogue with the teachers' and lawyers' associations - which were leading the civil disobedience campaign - soon fell apart and the government reacted by banning the associations, arresting, and jailing its leaders. Allegations of gross human rights violations on the part of security and defense operatives began to emerge. And these violations helped deepen the crisis further, making a non-violent, political settlement almost impossible. As all these were unfolding, both houses of Parliament - the National Assembly and the Senate - remained indolent.

One of the main constitutional responsibilities of the National Assembly is to control government action. As the elected representatives of the people, and by that token imbued with the political agency to act on their behalf, one would have expected parliament to step up in the heat of the crisis to check government excesses, redirect and re-orientate action. Astute political leadership at this time required of both houses of parliament to set-up fact-finding committees, tour the Anglophone regions, conduct independent hearings, listen to the grievances of their constituents and make recommendations to the government on how to address them. In the National Assembly, the Speaker and the CPDM caucus (including its Anglophones members) flatly refused to hold any form of debate on the conflict in Anglophone Cameroon. Attempts by the minority opposition parties, led by the SDF, to force a debate on the floor of the House were stymied by the Speaker and the majority CPDM. To this day, neither the National Assembly nor the Senate have held any formal debates on the conflict in Anglophone or passed as much as a non-binding resolution. This is a collective dereliction of political leadership and a negation of the principles of political agency. I could go further to say it is simply pusillanimity of another caliber.

Katherine Morton writes of leadership as "a social process of bargaining, negotiation, and persuasion to achieve a common goal".[25] Unfortunately none of these –bargaining, negotiation and persuasion – are hallmarks of Cameroonian political leadership. Cameroon's political leaders seem to believe that to bargain or to negotiate with, or to try to persuade, its citizens holding a view contrary to theirs is a sign of weakness. The default option of Cameroonian authorities

---

25   Ibid, p. 481.

in dealing with any form of popular dissent is to crack down on the dissenters. Seeking peaceful and non-violent approaches to managing dissent and mitigating conflicts has never been the forte of Cameroonian political leadership.

The Cameroonian nation is, without a modicum of doubt, in a leadership quandary. Collectively, the nation seems to be facing a leadership deficit at all levels. There is little trust and mutual respect left between those who identify as political leaders and their constituents or followers. Pervasive corruption has also served to erode the moral authority of the nation's political leadership. And any form of leadership that is exercised without the highest levels of morality, is simply coerced or baseless.

How then do we, as a nation and a people, reconstruct a leadership model that matches the task of renewing this nation for future generations?

Towards a People-Centered Leadership Paradigm

At the beginning of this chapter, I lauded the bold, audacious and transformational leadership style of the rulers of Dubai, which has led to the transformation of a desert outpost into one of the most prosperous and futuristic cities on earth. The example of Dubai can serve as our starting point. We can also draw inspiration from the vision of Botswana's founding President, Sir Seretse Khama - a vision that transformed Botswana from one of the poorest countries in Africa into an upper middle income economy enjoying steady economic growth, high standards of living and political stability.

Back to the Basics: Reinforcing Group Identity and Cohesion

We need to go back to the basics of good political leadership, which Barbara Kellerman defines as the ability of political leaders to *"create meaning and goals; reinforce group identity and cohesion; provide order; and mobilize collective work"*.[26] The people need to be put back at the center of any leadership endeavor. In that regard political leadership should be, and must be, about improving the lives of the citizenry through better and enhanced service delivery, listening to and then addressing their concerns in a timely manner, creating a propitious and enabling environment for the citizens of this country to reach their full potentials. This is the test that any one aspiring to a position of political leadership must henceforth pass.

Leadership comes alive in a group dynamic. Therefore, by definition,

---

26 Cited in Stéphane Langlais *The Meaning of Leadership in Political Systems*, Linnaeus University, 2014, p. 49.

leadership is a collective endeavor. You cannot lead a people without them. I stress this point because the top-down, autocratic, transactional leadership model (enabled by the heavily centralized state structure) that has existed in this country since unification in 1961 has run its course and needs to be replaced. Replacing this will entail shifting the focus from "Administration" to "Leadership". This country needs leaders, not administrators. This takes me back to Joseph Masciulli et al's government- leadership interconnection that I alluded to earlier in this chapter. The palpable lack of transformational political leadership has left the nation's public administration and institutions bereft of any sense of creativity and innovation. Any organization that ceases to innovate, easily slumps into routinized and repetitive administrative patterns, or simply put, inertia. President Biya himself has, on several occasions, decried the inertia that plagues the country's public administration system. It is not hard to fathom what causes this inertia: it is simply weak political leadership at all levels of the State apparatus. As Joseph Masciulli et al, aver, weak and unwise leadership contributes to government failures and can even bring about catastrophes. This country already suffers from the debilitating effects of different breeds of catastrophes: the catastrophe of tribalism, the catastrophe of corruption, the catastrophe of bad governance, the catastrophe of socio-economic stagnation, the catastrophe of identity politics, and, more poignantly, the catastrophe of an inept autocratic leadership.

Nursing Future Transformational Leaders and "Decentralized" Leadership

We cannot wait until our young people get into positions of power and authority before we start talking to them about the benefits of transformational leadership. Young Cameroonians must be inspired to exercise sterling leadership roles from school. This can be done through genuine, functional, but democratically elected student governments at all levels, where young people are given the opportunity to showcase their leadership potentials. Leadership, as a social science and as an academic discipline also needs to be part of the curriculum of all institutions of higher learning and professional training in Cameroon, beginning with the National School of Administration and Magistracy (ENAM), which trains the bulk of the nation's public managers. ENAM typically trains administrators not aspiring leaders, at least when I was there.

Outside the educational environment, we must make an effort to identify and leverage the abilities of young emerging leaders, by involving them in leadership roles at all levels, including outside the official structures of the state. I am thinking about village development associations, youth groups, civic engagement groups, religious groups etc. On a wider scale, Cameroon's decentralization process may not amount to much if it does not create favorable conditions for a transformational, political leadership to emerge and prosper within the institutions of governance, the institutions of the rule of law and within the public administration at regional and local level. In a sense, effective decentralization ought to result in the redistribution of power within the formal structures of the State. This can be achieved by encouraging and rewarding civic and social entrepreneurship, which should in turn elicit a sense of innovation, collective action and enhanced creativity at all levels of the State.

Conclusion

Innovation and creativity, anchored on a solid transformational leadership paradigm, are important prerequisites for renewing this nation and for moving it forward. Rule by strongmen must now give way to democratic governance, driven by visionary leadership. At some point the rulers of this country will have to come to the realization that bargaining, negotiation, persuasion and dialogue are critical leadership tools that must inform their everyday decision making, especially in moments of profound crisis. They are not a sign of weakness, but an expression of excellent political leadership. They exude respect, mutual concern, and above all else, a willingness to act in pursuit of the collective good.

Earlier on in this chapter, I cited examples of leaders whose out-of-the-box thinking and concern for the wellbeing of their communities led to innovations in the fields of education, agriculture, fish-farming and community saving and loan schemes. The Fish-Farming Station of Bome-Mbengwi, PNEU of Yaoundé, the GCE Board, the Credit Union League and Greenhouse Ventures are the enduring legacies of leaders and social entrepreneurs like Hon Gwen Burnley, Azong Wara and TAC, Pa Yasom Tondo, Roland Fomundam, and B.T Banseka.

When I look at the quality of this country's political leadership and its ruling elite, it is difficult, given the state of the country, to say with any measure of certitude, what their legacy to this nation is, or shall be. It worries me. I am sure it should worry them too. But it is not too late. We can turn things round by collectively embracing a transformational, policy-driven political leadership model, and using it as one of the tools for correcting the mistakes of the past sixty years. It should also serve to lay the groundwork for the renewal of this nation based on the dreams, the visions and the promise of its founders.

Chapter Six

Conclusion: Looking Ahead with Optimism

October 2021 marks the 60th anniversary of the unification of the French Cameroon and Southern Cameroons to form the Federal Republic of Cameroon. For all intents and purposes, it is also the 60th anniversary of the "independence by joining" of Southern Cameroons. This milestone demands an introspection and a stock-taking of our collective achievements and failures as a people and as a nation with a common destiny. This is part of what I set out to do in this treatise.

Mitigated Progress in an Autocratic State

There is no gainsaying the fact that Cameroon made significant strides in its economic and social development endeavors during the first two and the half decades after unification. Its mixed economy model, moored on a policy of Planned Liberalism, implemented through five-year development programs created the enabling conditions for growth and broad-based social development to take root. The one-party authoritarian state model also guaranteed a relatively stable political environment conducive for enhanced socio-economic advancement. There were laudable attempts to forge a sense of national unity and shared prosperity. Corruption and public waste were minimal. The quality of education and professional training was relatively higher and better than in comparable countries. Civil Service performance and public service delivery were commendable, in spite of many shortcomings. As a result, two decades after unification, Cameroon had already achieved the status of a lower middle income country, with better economic indicators than some East Asian countries, including some of those that came to be known as the East Asian Tigers. But these laudable advances in economic and social development came at a great cost. Under President Ahidjo's one-man, highhanded rule, dissent in all its forms were not tolerated; individual and collective freedoms were severely curtailed; respect for human rights and the rule of law were not State priorities. Cameroon was in all material respects, a quintessential police state where the arbitrary arrest, torture and prolonged detention, often without trial, of political dissidents and all others considered a threat to the "security of the state", was common place. This notwithstanding, it is safe to say that by the time Mr. Amadou Ahidjo stepped down as President and Head of State in November 1982 (after more than two decades) Cameroon was considered politically stable and with high prospects and potentials of achieving economic prosperity and social advancement.

So as can be expected, President Biya's New Deal era came with a lot of promise, predicated on the foundation Ahidjo had laid. President Biya's early years in office were marked by internecine political disputes between himself and his predecessor (1983 to 1985), a grueling economic crisis that led to the lost decade of the mid '80s to the mid '90s and socio-political disorder aggravated by a bungled process of the return to multi-party politics (1990). The situation was further compounded by rampant corruption, misgovernance, maladministration, a botched, half-hearted democratization and liberalization process, political and social instability and the resurgence of an inert, intolerant, repressive, authoritarian state. The result has been stagnation and the somewhat mitigated progress in the nation's development efforts.

Recent Efforts to enhance Growth and Development

If the government is not reaching its socio-economic development and structural reform goals, it is not for lack of effort. From unification in 1961 to the advent of the economic crisis in 1985, Cameroon developed and implemented a total of six five-year development plans. The five-year development planning model gave way to a string of structural adjustment programs that were developed to address the economic crisis of the mid-80s. After reaching the completion point of the Heavily Indebted Poor Countries (HIPC) Initiative, the focus shifted from structural adjustment to poverty reduction. In 2003 the government produced its first Poverty Reduction Strategy Paper (PRSP). In 2007, the third Cameroon Household Survey (known by its French acronym ECAM) revealed unsatisfactory results in the fight against poverty. The PRSP had clearly not attained its stated objectives and so needed to be revised. Thus, a twenty five-year development program dubbed "Vision 2035" was adopted in 2009 to serve as the reference framework and the country's socio-economic development strategy for the period 2010 to 2035. A Growth and Employment Strategy Paper (GESP) was also developed as the main implementation instrument of the first decade (2010 to 2019) of Vision 2035.

As I stated in Chapter Two, Vision 2035 and the GESP were very clear and articulate in their goals. The overall goal of Vision 2035 is to make Cameroon an emerging, democratic country united in its diversity. In this regard, the Vision aims to (i) reduce poverty to a socially acceptable level; (ii) lift Cameroon to the status of a medium-income country; enable Cameroon to achieve the status of a Newly Industrialized Country; and (iv) reinforce national unity and consolidate the democratic process. The GESP was more specific and quantitative in its own goals. Its focus was on accelerating growth, creating formal employment and reducing poverty. In that regard, it aimed to: i) increase annual growth rate to 5.5% between 2010 and 2020, ii) reduce underemployment rate from 75.8% to less than 50% in 2020 through the creation of thousands of formal positions year-on-year over ten years, iii) reduce income poverty rate from 39.9% in 2007 to 28.7 % in 2020.

The implementation of the GESP ended in December 2019 and according to the government's own evaluation, its goals too were not entirely met. With regard to GDP growth, the government assessed that:

> ... the implementation of the GESP has made it possible to boost growth from 3.0 percent during the PRSP period to 4.5 percent during the 2010-2019 period. This average growth, which was nonetheless 0.8 points below the 5.5% target set in the GESP, nevertheless affirms the resilience of the Cameroonian economy in the face of various economic and security shock.[1]

With regard to reducing underemployment and poverty, the government assessed that *"the situation of underemployment has worsened and the income poverty rate has fallen only marginally"*.[2] Corruption in government continues to spiral out of control and the business climate remains largely unfavorable to external and domestic investment. Some of the reasons given for this inadequate performance includes the armed conflict in the Anglophone Regions, the Boko Haram insurgency in the northern part of the country and the spillover effects of the armed conflict in the Central African Republic.

In November 2020, the government launched a new development program to replace the GESP. This new program was dubbed the "National Development

1   National Development Strategy 2020, p.1.
2   Ibid, p.24.

Strategy 2030" (or NDS30 for short). NDS2030 is the second phase of the implementation of Cameroon Vision 2035 and shall run from 2020 to 2030. Its overall objectives are to: i) establish conditions favorable to economic growth and accumulation of national wealth and ensure that the structural changes indispensable for the industrialization of the country are achieved; (ii) to improve on the living conditions of the population and their access to basic social services by ensuring a significant reduction in poverty and underemployment; (iii) to strengthen climate change adaptation and mitigate the effects of climate change and ensure environmental management that assures sustainable and inclusive economic growth and social development; and (iv) to improve on governance to enhance policy performance towards achieving development goals. The government hopes to achieve these objectives through, i) a structural transformation of the national economy, ii) the development of human capital and wellbeing, iii) promotion of employment and economic integration, iv) enhanced governance, decentralization and strategic management of the State. The strategy emphasizes Import Substitution Industrialization as the engine that will drive growth, create formal high-paying jobs, and reduce poverty and inequalities. It remains to be seen if the implementation of NDS30 shall be more successful than that of the other development programs that came before it.

Unlocking the Development Logjam

So why is it that for the last twenty-five or so years the government has been unable to satisfactorily implement its own development programs or to achieve its social transformation agenda? This is also the question that this treatise set out to answer. And the answer is a very simple one. It is a phenomenon best explained by the proverbial pouring of new wine into old wine skins. Implementing new development programs within the same old governance frameworks that have outlived their usefulness and are ill-adapted to the exigencies of a modern society is susceptible to producing a fairly predictable result: mitigated success. As I noted in the opening chapters of this book, Cameroon's inert, inept, heavy, over-centralized Jacobin-state model has outlived its usefulness. It is the one thing most responsible for the country's current institutional and development logjam.

In this book I have proposed common sense, three-prong, overarching, governance-based proposals for unlocking this logjam. These proposals can also serve as the entry points for the refoundation of this nation, based on the vision and the promises of its founders. These proposals are again summarized below.

First, we need to untangle our decentralization conundrum. This can be done through a truly decentralized governance system where regional governors and regional legislative councils elected by direct suffrage are exercising a wide range of constitutionally-mandated executive and legislative functions. Ideally, this should lead to a redistribution of power and responsibilities, such that the development of this nation is not left in the hands of a patently corrupt few but is evenly shared among all its citizens operating at the different levels of the state structure. Also, a truly decentralized governance system, based on the historical heritage of Anglophone Cameroon (self-reliance, self-actualization, self-government, citizen voice, ownership and accountability) could best address the Anglophone Problem and the Southern Cameroons Question.

Second, decentralized governance must necessarily be complemented by enhance public service delivery. Drawing inspiration from the principles of New Public Management and Reinventing Government, it is imperative to reform and rethink public service provisioning in this country so as to enhance government's capacity to deliver services to the population in a timely, efficient, effective and economical manner. This should be possible through a new governing architecture in which the Central Government assumes a more strategic or steering role like planning and programming, oversight and control, setting and ensuring compliance with norms and standards. The Regional Governments on their part will play a more operational (or rowing) role in basic service delivery and the promotion of grassroots socio-economic development. Furthermore, leveraging and harnessing civic and social entrepreneurship, enforcing public accountability measures and embracing e-governance should serve as critical building blocks for an enhanced public service delivery system.

Lastly, moving this country forward and re-imagining and rebuilding it from the bottom up requires a different political leadership model. There is therefore the imperious need to make a paradigmatic shift from the present top-down, transactional political leadership style to a political leadership model that is transformational, bold, innovative and audacious and which places the needs and wellbeing of the citizenry at the center of all its endeavors; a political leadership style that is receptive to the notions of civic and social entrepreneurship. Simply put, this country needs bold and innovative leaders to take it to the next level, not rulers incapable of ridding themselves of their innate bureaucratic impulses. This will entail also making a strategic shift from "Administration" to "Leadership" and inculcating into young Cameroonians the enduring qualities of transformational leadership during their formative years, both within and outside the formal educational structures.

Tackling the Southern Cameroons Question and Anglophone Problem

The refoundation of the Cameroon nation must also adequately and genuinely address the grievances of Anglophone Cameroonians, with a view to correcting the injustices that have been visited on them since 1961. No matter how we see it, the rise and the persistence of Anglophone Cameroon Nationalism is the direct consequence of the brazen travesty of the Promise of Foumban, and the subsequent inability of the government to live up to the Promise of 20 May 1972 and the Promise of the New Deal. As the armed, violent conflict presently raging in the North-West and South-West Regions has shown, and in spite of efforts over the years to undermine and minimize it, Anglophone Cameroon Nationalism is not going away anytime soon. The Southern Cameroons Question and the Anglophone Problem stem from a perception among Anglophone Cameroonians that their self-determination process was either botched or derailed and is therefore incomplete. The consequence has been their assimilation and marginalization within the wider Cameroonian polity. A half-baked, insincere decentralization process, implemented almost perfunctorily cannot be the solution to the Southern Cameroons Question and the Anglophone Problem. Neither is the so-called "Special Status". And the solution cannot also be found in "Ambazonia", or at least not in the version of it that emerged after 2016.

Let me explain why.

In the preceding chapters I already stated why I think the current decentralization process and the "special status" are inadequate as mechanisms or policy frameworks for addressing deep-rooted and entrenched Anglophone Cameroon grievances and the injustices Anglophones have suffered in the past and continue to suffer to this day. To recap, the General Code of Regional and Local Authorities offers very little in terms novelty. It merely recoups different decentralization frameworks that had existed in the country before. The high level of Central Government control over, and intrusion in the affairs of the Region, as well as the subordination of the elected Chairperson of the Regional Council to the authority of the Governor (an appointed bureaucrat), render the Special Status meaningless. It is nothing but a replication of the infuriatingly reprehensible plot by Ahidjo in the 1960s to undermine the elected government of West Cameroon by placing it under the authority of a Federal Inspector of Administration (an appointed bureaucrat). Anglophones resented it then and they resent it now.

I also do not believe that another political union between the North-West and the South-West (as existed between 1954 and 1972), within an independent state of whatever name or contraption, is still sustainable or even feasible. In saying so I am not in any manner, shape or form discounting the decades-long struggle of Anglophone Cameroonians for justice, equal treatment and the end to marginalization. A struggle for which many have died and continue to die. The problem with the Anglophone/Southern Cameroons Struggle is that it has always been very regressive in thought and rather backward-looking in nature. It is being waged as if time is frozen in a set mathematical formula. It seems as if the successive leaders of the struggle - from those of the Southern Cameroons National Council (SCNC) of the 90s to those of today rallying around the "Ambazonia" concept - never envisaged an outcome that takes into account the passage of time and the changes to our national character that it has engendered. As far as I am concerned, it serves no strategic purpose to continue to define the self-determination struggle of Anglophone Cameroon in terms of what existed in the past, as if sixty years of unification with *La Republique du Cameroun* have counted for nothing. The past, no matter how glamorous and glorious remains the past. While it can serve as a compass to map out the future, that future cannot be wholly predicated on it. That is why a re-fashioning, a rehashing or a reenactment of Southern/West Cameroon is too regressive to serve as a viable solution to the Southern Cameroons Question and the Anglophone Problem. I believe that henceforth, Anglophone Cameroon's struggle for self-determination and its fight against continuous marginalization and the status of second-class citizenship within the Cameroon nation-state can be successfully waged within the current 10-region framework. For, ultimately, what Anglophone Cameroonians are demanding is the recognition of their inalienable right as a people to freely govern themselves, within a governing structure that guarantees the preservation of their shared values and common identity derived from their historical heritage. And they want to do so in a manner consistent with the promise made to their forebears in Foumban in 1961; the promise to build a unique nation, federal in character but united in its diversity and in purpose; proud of its bicultural heritage derived from the distinct colonial, historical and cultural realities of each of the two parts of the union. That is why it is important, at least conceptually, not to conflate and confuse the legitimate, non-violent and historical struggle for self-determination of Anglophone/Southern Cameroons with the "Ambazonia Struggle", especially the version of it that was revealed to the world after 2016. "Ambazonia" shall pass, no doubt about that, but the struggle for self-determination and the restoration of the dignity of the people of Southern Cameroons, buoyed by their sense of righteous indignation, shall endure forever. I however, feel the need at this point to raise a caveat here.

From what I have seen so far of this latest version of Ambazonia, I fear the freedom-seeking people of Southern Cameroons might already be trapped between two Pharaohs – one on either side of the Red Sea with the people in between, pummeled by unrelenting waves and unsure of which of the Pharaohs to turn to for deliverance.

I must vehemently stress that there shall never be a purely military solution to the armed conflict in Anglophone Cameroon. I foresee a scenario where, over time, both sides - government forces and armed separatists - shall fight each other to a stalemate. It does not seem to me that, in the short and medium term, the government shall be able to regain full civil and military control of the entirety of the North-West and South-West regions. I also do not believe that the armed separatists shall ever be able to militarily takeover the whole of the North-West and South-West Regions, or to establish an alternative civil administration or parallel governance structures in those two regions. As the conflict drags on with no end in sight, local military commanders and local separatists fighters shall enter into informal "non-aggression pacts", purely as a means of surviving in the battlefield. What shall ensue then will be a low intensity but deadly armed conflict, lasting decades, with devastating consequences on civilian life and property.

I can also say that the political underpinnings of the "Ambazonia Struggle", if ever there was one, are gradually being eroded. Armed separatists groups are fast morphing into criminal gangs, driven by the financial and economic benefits that come with armed conflict: extortion, kidnapping for ransom, forceful expropriation of private and public property, armed/highway robbery, illicit trade and trafficking of sorts. In the process, gross human rights abuses such as rapes, murders, torture, gratuitous killings, illegal detentions and other forms of violent crime shall continue unabated and with impunity. This is the predictable outcome of a "struggle" which, from the start, was bereft of a manifesto, a doctrinal foundation and a clear statement of intent.

Similarly, if corrupt and unscrupulous government officials and senior military commanders are benefitting financially from the conflict as alleged, they shall see no point in working to end it.

The conflict shall continue to disproportionately affect the poorer and more vulnerable sections of the civilian population. About 80 per cent of the economy of the NW and SW Regions is in the informal sector. It is essentially an economy of small traders and farmers. And this is the sector that has been worse hit. A recent World Bank assessment of the conflict speaks of deepening poverty, desperation, and the gradual erosion of Anglophone Cameroon's socio-economic fabric. This too shall take decades to repair.[3] However, the human cost of the conflict in those two regions may never be recovered.

A Resilient Economy in the Midst of Conflict?

The above notwithstanding, Cameroon's economy seems to be holding its own. The joint World Bank/IMF 2020 Debt Sustainability Analysis assessed Cameroon's risk of debt distress as HIGH. However, its granularity rating was assessed as sustainable.[4] Cameroon's debt-to-GDP ratio for 2021 stands at 42 per cent and is projected to decrease to 35 percent by 2026. This is still more than 30 points below the World Bank recommended threshold of 77 per cent debt-to-GDP ratio. Annual inflation remained stable at 1.6 per cent well below the CEMAC convergence criteria of 3 per cent. With debt stock indicators well below the recommended thresholds, stable inflation, a renegotiated Eurobond maturity date, strategic commodities like oil and minerals untouched by the conflict, and a projected average GDP growth rate of 4.3 per cent in the medium term (2019-2024), the fundamentals of Cameroon's economy can be said to be still strong, despite the crisis.

With such somewhat encouraging numbers, I suspect the government will continue to defer the search for a durable, peaceful, non-military solution to the conflict. A separatist leader told me that during a meeting with the government, an official told him that the Cameroon government has the resources and the time to fight the separatists for eternity. Maybe it is this somewhat favorable economic outlook that drives this mindset. Nonetheless, as everyone knows, even the best of economies can still be subjected to shocks. The World Bank report I alluded to above, in its assessment of the conflict in Anglophone Cameroon, says GDP growth could slow by as much as 9 percent if the conflict drags on to 2025.

The Imperative of Seeking a Political Settlement to the Anglophone Conflict

The Southern Cameroons Question and the Anglophone Problem are political issues that require well thought-out, sincere, comprehensive, political solutions. And to achieve this will require sterling leadership and good faith from the Yaoundé ruling elite and from those who have arrogated onto themselves the mantle of leadership within the Anglophone Cameroon community. It shall demand compromise from both sides. This compromise could proceed from the

---

3   World Bank. 2021, "The Socio-Political Crisis in the Northwest and Southwest Regions of Cameroon: Assessing the Economic and Social Impacts". World Bank, Washington, DC.

4   Joint World Bank-IMF Debt Sustainability Analysis, January 2021, pp. 1-3.

realization that the right to self-determination does not always necessarily result in statehood. Above all else, it shall entail the dismantling of the structures of violence, so that we can end the conflict and also win the peace. My preferred approach to ending the violence in Anglophone Cameroon has been to explore ways and means of how we can collectively, as one people under one nation, do better instead of asking who is to blame.

Finding a lasting solution to the Southern Cameroons Question and to the Anglophone Problem is critical to the survival of this nation and to the renewal of the promises that have defined it for the past six decades.

We rise or we fall as a Collective

I am aware that this treatise overwhelmingly paints a picture of Cameroon as a country where very few things seem to work. This is only partly true. My aim here has been to factually and statistically show where we have fallen behind as a nation and then to make concrete proposals on how we can pick ourselves up and march on again. This treatise is not an indictment of anybody. Our failures and shortcomings have been collective. And it is only as a collective that we can rise again and take on the challenge of reforming, refounding and rebuilding this nation from the bottom up, based on its promises.

Nevertheless, to do this shall require a sincere effort on our part to recognize that we, as a nation, are not where we ought to be. Conventional wisdom holds that the first step to resolving a problem is to recognize that there is one. Such a recognition should galvanize us towards renewing our commitment to make this country strong, prosperous, democratic and united in its diversity. And I know we can do it. Cameroon is blessed with immense human and natural resource potentials. We may disagree. We may never arrive at a consensus on issues of national importance. However, the things that bind and unite us as Cameroonians far outweigh, and are far more important than the things that separate and divide us. We cannot continue to allow unscrupulous politicians and individuals of bad faith to play up our little differences. We can stop them by emphasizing and projecting our collective strength. Our Cameroonicity - by which I mean those inscrutable bonds that connect us - is more profound than we know. Our union is not perfect, no doubt about that, but we have it within our power to make it better. Collectively we can make the promise of this nation, a promise of success.

That is why I look at the future of this great country with unfettered optimism. I trust in the resilience of the valiant men and women of this nation. And it is that trust that leads me to believe that we can and we will overcome the governance inadequacies and leadership quandary that has plagued this nation for the past six decades. It behooves of this generation to renew the promises on which this nation was founded and built, so that this land can truly become that "land of promise" and that "land of glory" we speak of in our National Anthem.

Bibliography

Acemoglu, D., & Robinson, J. A. (2012). *Why Nations Fail: The Origins of Power, Prosperity and Poverty*. New York: Crown.

Al Maktoum, M. b. R. (2012). *My vision: challenges in the race for excellence*. Dubai: Motivate Publishing.

Bass, B. M., & Avolio, B. J. (Eds.). (1994). *Improving organizational effectiveness through transformational leadership*. Thousand Oaks, CA, US: Sage Publications, Inc.

Burns, J. M. (1978). *Leadership*. New York: Harper & Row.

Collier, P. (2007). *The Bottom Billion: Why Poor Countries are Failing and what can be done about It*. Oxford: Oxford University Press.

Dimier, V. (2004). On Good Colonial Government: Lessons from the League of Nations. *Global Society, 18*(3), 279-299.

Dinka, G. (1985). *The New Social Order*. Yaounde.

Duguit, L. (1923). The Concept of Public Service. *Yale Law Journal, 32*(5).

Faguet, J.-P., Fox, A. M., & Poeschl, C. (2014). *Does decentralization strengthen or weaken the state? Authority and social learning in a supple state*. London School of Economics and Political Science, London, UK: Department of International Development.

Gellner, E. (1983). *Nations and Nationalism*. Oxford: Basil Blackwell Publisher Limited.

Guiake, M., & Tianzue, Z. (2019). Higher Education's Curriculum and Challenges of the 21st Century: The Case Study of Cameroonian Public Universities. *Journal of Education and Practice, 10*(18), 123.

Hood, C. (1991). A Public Management for All Seasons? *Public Administration, 69*(1), 3-19.

Kofele-Kale, N. (2011). Local governance under Cameroon's decentralisation regime: is it all sound and fury signifying nothing? *Commonwealth Law Bulletin, 37*(3), 513-530.

Langlais, S. (2014). *The Meaning of Leadership in Political Systems*. (Independent thesis Advanced level (degree of Master (One Year)) Student thesis), Retrieved from http://urn.kb.se/resolve?urn=urn:nbn:se:lnu:diva-34711 DiVA database.

Leadbeater, C., & Goss, S. (1998). *Civic Entrepreneurship*. London: Demos.

Lugard, L. (1922). *The Dual Mandate in British Tropical Africa*. London: Frank Case and Co Ltd.

Mamdani, M. (2004). *Citizen and Subject: Contemporary Africa and the Legacy of Late Colonialism*. Kampala: Fountain Publishers.

Masciulli, J., Molchanov, M. A., & Knight, W. A. (2009). Political Leadership in Context.

In J. Masciulli, M. A. Molchanov, & W. A. Knight (Eds.), *The Ashgate Research Companion to Political Leadership*. London & New York: Routledge.

Maundeni, Z., Mpabanga, D., & Mfundisi, A. (2007). *Consolidating Democratic Governance in Southern Africa: Botswana.*

Miller, K. (2002). *Advantages and Disadvantages of Local Government Decentralization.* Paper presented at the Caribbean Conference on Local Government and Decentralization, Georgetown, Guyana.

Morton, K. (2017). Political Leadership and Global Governance: Structural Power Versus Custodial Leadership. *Chinese Political Science Review, 2*(4), 477-493.

Nde, C. J., Raymond, A., Saidu, Y., Cheng, N. I., Nzuobontane, D., Atemnkeng, J. T., & Mbacham, W. F. (2019). Reaching universal health coverage by 2035: is cameroon on track. *Universal Journal of Public Health, 7*(3), 110-117.

Ndi, A. (2016). *The Golden Age of Southern Cameroons: Vital Lessons for Cameroon*. Denver: Spears Media Press.

Ngoh, V. J. (2019). *Cameroon 1884-Present (2018): The History of a People*. Limbe: Design House.

Northouse, P. G. (2013). *Leadership Theory and Practice,* Los Angeles: SAGE Publications

Osborne, D., & Gaebler, T. (1992). *Reinventing government: How the entrepreneurial spirit is transforming the public sector.* New York: Addison-Wesley.

Page, B. (2003). Communities as the agents of commodification: The Kumbo Water Authority in Northwest Cameroon. *Geoforum, 34*(4), 483-498.

Reid, W. M., & Dold, C. J. (2018). Burns, Senge, and the Study of Leadership. *Open Journal of Leadership, 7*(1), 89-116.

Rice, S. E., & Patrick, S. (2008). *Index of State Weakness in the Developing World*. Retrieved from The Brookings Institution, Washington, DC.

Sachs, J. (2005). *The End of Poverty: Economic Possibilities of our Times*. New York: Penguin Books.

Sebudubudu, D., & Botlhomilwe, M. Z. (2012). The critical role of leadership in Botswana's development: What lessons? *Leadership, 8*(1), 29-45.

Tambi, M. D. (2015). Economic Growth, Crisis, and Recovery in Cameroon: A Literature Review. *Journal of Industrial Distribution & Business, 6*(1), 5-15.

Tendler, J. (1997). *Good Government in the Tropics*: Johns Hopkins University Press.

Thompson, F. J., & Riccucci, N. M. (1998). Reinventing Government. *Annual Review of Political Science, 1*(1), 231-257.

Tracey, J. B., & Hinkin, T. R. (1998). Transformational Leadership or Effective Managerial Practices? *Group & Organization Management, 23*(3), 220-236.

INDEX

www.ingramcontent.com/pod-product-compliance
Lightning Source LLC
Chambersburg PA
CBHW072134020426
42334CB00018B/1799